క

"Especially valuable during a time of global economic uncertainty that affects all leaders and businesses - small and large - the 7 Steps provides invaluable insights across a set of timely topics. Marilyn's coaching expertise provides guidance in a manner that focuses on you, the reader. She has uniquely assembled wisdoms from great leadership thinkers in a simple to understand and actionable set of stories and exercises. A must read for today's times."

David G. Thomson

Business Advisor to Growth Companies and author of *Blueprint to a Billion: 7 Essentials to Achieve Exponential Growth*

క

"For all the small business owners out there who are struggling in these times, Marilyn McLeod has written a primer you MUST read. It contains heartfelt and hard-won wisdom for all who want to get beyond the mass of information and infomercials they receive every day. This book literally is brimming with enthusiasm while offering clear ideas for success.'

'In this book Marilyn offers practical steps for anyone who wants to start or grow their own business. She does so in a way that is principled as well as reflective. While she channels wisdom from Marshall Goldsmith to Nathaniel Branden, her real contribution is to the business owner. Her 7 principles resonate with the concept that YOU are the most important engine of growth for your own enterprise, and she offers guidance for how you should best spend your precious time, as well as how to think beyond the present in overcoming challenges and obstacles. She offers some great stories to support her points, while keeping the perspective of a coach who is there to help you."

James Goodrich

Founding Dean, Marshall Goldsmith School of Management, Alliant International University

"I have known and worked with Marilyn for almost 10 years. She has always surrounded herself and learned from an eclectic group of the best thought leaders. In her very timely book she shares her personal journey and the journey of others to knowledge and towards wisdom in a very usable way. All we need is the courage, commitment, and discipline to use blueprint she lays out in her wonderful book.

Chris Coffey
Keynote Speaker, Leadership Educator, Executive Coach

"Intuitive wisdom made practical!"

Kim A. Gutner, M.D., DFAPA
Child, Adolescent and Adult Psychiatry

"Martin Luther King Jr. once said, 'The ultimate measure of a man is not where he stands in moments of comfort and convenience, but where he stands at times of challenge and controversy'.'

'In *Recession or Plenty: 7 Steps to Success in Business & in Life*, Marilyn courageously shares with us her past personal challenges, and like Phoenix rising from the ashes, provides a road map you can immediately use to be successful in your personal and business life. Marilyn serves as your personal coach by first helping you define the person within you, therefore making it easier to create the world you so desire around you. A must read!"

James Singletary
All-American, former NFL Linebacker, now a Behavioral Optometrist and OrthoKeratologist

"Extremely moving, inspiring, heart-wrenching, great!"

Nathaniel Branden
Psychotherapist and philosopher author of twenty books on the psychology of self-esteem, romantic love, and the life and thought of Objectivist philosopher Ayn Rand.

ॐ

"*Recession or Plenty: 7 Steps to Success in Business & in Life* is a valuable guidebook for all of us on our journey to success, however we define it. The questions the book asks are almost more valuable than the answers provided. And the exercises help move us into the future that we will redefine, in our own way, after taking *Recession or Plenty* … to heart."

Frances Hesselbein
Chairman of the Board of Governors of the Leader to Leader Institute, was the Founding President of the Peter F. Drucker Foundation and was CEO of the Girl Scouts of the USA, 1976-1990. Mrs. Hesselbein was awarded the Presidential Medal of Freedom, the United States of America's highest civilian honor, in 1998 by President Clinton. In 2002 Mrs. Hesselbein was the first recipient of the Dwight D. Eisenhower National Security Series Award for her service "to national security and the nation". She is the author of *Hesselbein on Leadership*, and *Be, Know, Do: Leadership the Army Way*, introduced by Frances and General Eric K. Shinseki.

ॐ

"Marilyn's book follows a principle I use in my work: A concept distilled into its simplest form saves everyone valuable time. Her book is small enough to carry around, yet carries the weight of great thinkers and concepts that not only make sense intellectually, but have also been proven to work. She has created a practical, useful tool full of helpful ideas which are balanced with practical how-to exercises and useful questions.

The tone of the book is friendly. It is like having Marilyn in the room. Give yourself ten minutes here, half an hour there, and read her book as an idea-generator for whatever issues you are facing. With wisdom distilled from her coaching practice, Marilyn's got it right. She clearly has her finger on the pulse of what you need to know today to manage yourself in a small business.

Marshall Goldsmith

www.MarshallGoldsmithLibrary.com
Marshall is a world authority in helping successful leaders get even better – by achieving positive, lasting change in behavior: for themselves, their people and their teams. He is also a *New York Times, Wall Street Journal, BusinessWeek, USAToday* and *Publisher's Weekly* best-selling author of *What Got You Here Won't Get You There* and *MOJO: How to Get It, How to Keep It, and How to Get it Back When You Need It!* , and *Succession: Are You Ready?*.

&

"As an entrepreneur running a small consultancy business, Marilyn's coaching has inspired me to carry on when things looked tough, and given me ideas for new ventures based on what's in my toolkit, interpreted with her help in whole new ways. Her assistance has been profoundly important to my overall success over the past few years.'

'Marilyn's book does something unique: It brings together some of the most valuable inspirational resources but also practical "nuts and bolts" knowledge that we all need. Her book is helping me in both ways to get through these very difficult times and reach my goals. I credit this book in helping me to thrive not just survive."

Gary Ranker

Forbes Top Five Executive Coach and author of *Political Dilemmas at Work*

"I know Marilyn and well enough that I can actually hear her voice in the book. And it is a refreshingly encouraging voice – never down, always warm and capable of making you see things that you knew but were unable to relate to your own circumstances till she showed you how.'

'She is self effacing but does not mince words and shows you very clearly what you have to do to junk the detritus you carry around with you – often without realizing it! – and start living a life where great things happen to you routinely, and where every day is a blast. This will not happen to you if you merely read the book. There is an excellent chance that it will happen to you if you actually do the things she so clearly and lovingly prescribes."

Srikumar S. Rao

Professor Srikumar Rao, author of *Are You Ready to Succeed?*, *Happiness at Work* and The Personal Mastery Program. His "Creativity and Personal Mastery" course has been so successful at London Business School, Columbia Business School, and Haas School of Business that it has its own alumni association.

Also by Marilyn McLeod:

Conscious Networking
Finding and Creating Your Ideal Communities

Nutrigenomic Diet for Weight and Fat Loss
One Consumer's Journey

Peer Coaching
Extending Your Coaching Dollar

Secrets of Self Publishing
Digital Tools for Publishing and Marketing

Recession or Plenty POCKET, ABRIDGED VERSION

Social Media Series:

Social Media for Beginners
Step by Step for Small Business

Social Media for Small Business
Tips for Using Your Time Effectively

How to Work with Your Web Developer
Asking the Right Questions

Social Media Strategy
Navigating the New World Online

Social Media Workbook
Creating Your Master Plan

Recession or Plenty

7 Steps to Success in Business & in Life

by Marilyn McLeod

Consider the Possibility Press
www.considerthepossibilitypress.com

Recession or Plenty:
7 Steps to Success in Business & in Life

Cover design by Jeff Kahn

For information:

Consider the Possibility Press
http://www.considerthepossibilitypress.com
P O Box 703
Cardiff-by-the-Sea, CA 92007 U.S.A.
+1-760-644-2284

Library of Congress Catalog Card Number

International Standard Book Number
978-0-9822290-2-6

Printed in the United States of America

7 Steps to Success

YOU
CUSTOMERS
BUSINESS
FOCUS
SALES
FOLLOW-UP
REVIEW

Dedication

I dedicate this book to Olaf Bolm and Rosalind de Mille who began their 78-year friendship when they met at age ten in Hollywood. They gave me a gift of seeing me and accepting me as I am. Though my parents' age, they lovingly included me in their lives as a trusted friend. Olaf, like his father Adolph Bolm, drew out of me the potential he saw by helping me become aware of what I was doing right, and kindly pointing out what detracted. He was proud to hear I was writing this book, as he encouraged me in any creative endeavor.

Rosalind's response to what I wrote above, "Good." Besides Mrs. Bolm, Rosalind knew Olaf and Adolph Bolm better than anyone. I had the privilege of watching Rosalind read through my first draft, hearing her giggle and watching her turn pages eagerly. She and Olaf both moved to the next experience beyond this life in the months before this book went to print.

Rosalind deMille and Olaf Bolm
July 23, 2001
in Carlsbad, California
Photo by Marilyn McLeod

Table of Contents

Section Four - Tools & Resources

Section Five - Reference

Acknowledgements

First and foremost, I want to acknowledge Marshall Goldsmith. Not only has he saved me years of developing my own coaching process by describing his concept of FeedForward and a guaranteed improvement coaching method when I first heard him speak in 2002, he's also been a wonderful role model as I find my own voice and pull together this resource for leaders.

Marshall and Lyda Goldsmith are a perfect complement to each other as a team, and are an absolute pleasure to work with. They live the principles of respect and clear, honest, nonjudgmental communication expressed in the coaching style I've learned from Marshall.

In addition, Marshall has introduced me to thought leaders and industry leaders who are giants in their field, including Paul Hersey, Frances Hesselbein, Alan Mulally, Nathaniel Branden, Ken Shelton, John Byrne, R. Roosevelt Thomas, Jr., Ken Blanchard, Gary Ranker, Jim Goodrich, Srikumar S. Rao, Joel Barker, Chris Coffey, David G. Thomson, Sally Helgeson, Cathy Greenberg, Steve Rodgers, Frank Wagner, Denise Sinuk and many others. Of course learning about the world from their point of view has been exceedingly enlightening and inspiring, and beyond that meeting them as people has been transformative. I thank each of them for their patience with me as I learn, their interest in me as a person, and their valuable contributions to this book, whether in person or in spirit.

When Ken Shelton offered to coach me through the process of writing a book, I thought it would be a straightforward process. I had an outline in mind and expected to simply fill in the blanks throughout the year. When I shared this perspective with Sally Helgeson, she just laughed and shook her head. So did Nathaniel Branden. It has been a much deeper experience than I expected. Ken changed the whole playing field when he said,

"Your book should be your perfect business card." That led me to a year of inner reflection as well as looking at what value I could contribute to the people I would like to work with in the future. Thank you so much, Ken, for expertly guiding me to this thought process which produced a much richer end product. Even more than that, thank you for the many times your words gave me a wonderful belly laugh at just the right moment!

Thank you also to Jeff Kahn for his wonderful cover design and his helpful ideas for the title, and to Anna Marie Valerio for turning it all upside down. Thank you Robert J. Lee for challenging me to put my own photo on my own book. Thank you Kevin Cashman for helping me find the fourth room and a level of comfort with my passion. Thank you Marshall Goldsmith for encouraging me to share my history. Thank you to Dr. Kim Gutner for reviewing my recommendations for children. Thank you Linda Olin-Weiss whose encouragement at the right moment helped me find my heart in the book. Thank you Sarah McArthur, Andrea Burgess and Beverly Barr for their editorial comments and to Kathryn Hall for giving the cover one more look.

As I read this list, I realize how far I've come through adversity. Earlier in my life I thought I had to do it all myself or I was weak or a failure, or at the very least an unwelcome burden. During this book project it's been so easy to ask and receive from these wonderful people who seem to enjoy contributing ... what a blessing! Yes, I'm so glad for my ability to improve and learn something new!!

A very special thank you to Arthur Samuel Joseph for believing in me, and for coaxing and cajoling my Self to risk engaging with life. And thank you to Jacqueline M. Welch for her generosity in being a mentor helping me find my authentic Self.

I also want to thank the many people who have contributed their voice to the larger world, whose efforts have given me stepping stones to find my way from a childhood with very few options even for survival to a happy adult life filled with possibility. This includes: Oprah, Rich de Vos and Jay Van Andel, Bill W. and Lois, John Muir, Barack Obama, Colin Powell, Al Quie, Gloria Steinem, Anna Pavlova and Adolph Bolm, Abraham Lincoln, Buckminster Fuller, Albert Schweitzer, Thomas Jefferson, Marshall Thurber, Marshall Rosenberg, the American pioneers, and the many who have written books and shared their spiritual path and experience to help lighten the way.

A friend who read my book said it kind of looked as though I was selling many of the people I mention in this book. I told him that was true, but not in the way he might think. I know the value of these concepts. They came from a variety of sources, and I hope the reader will reach for the original sources as needed.

I hope my book accurately reflects the views of my many mentors who have influenced my thinking, and I hope the finished book will be a useful tool for people in any capacity who choose to take an active role in creating a better life for themselves and those around them. My goal is to bring together the best tools I have at my disposal, and make them available to my readers in a very usable way.

Foreword

During my career, I have had the privilege of working with over 100 major CEO's and their management teams. My clients are already successful leaders who are working to "take it to the next level" and get even better.

I met Marilyn in 2002 when I was looking for someone to create a website for me. "Just a small website," I told her. Not only did she help me create my small website just the way I envisioned it, she also helped me grow it into a significant Internet presence that catalogs my work, and gives my clients and anyone who visits hundreds of articles, columns, videos and audios about the concepts I teach in my coaching practice.

Throughout the years we have worked together, Marilyn has applied her broad range of skills to several new projects and opportunities in my own business. She has shown the highest integrity and has handled a couple of tough situations in a very professional way.

Marilyn has firsthand experience with the Marshall Goldsmith coaching concepts she presents in her book. She recently managed a coaching engagement with four very senior executives in a 'Fortune 500' client of mine. She did a wonderful job of managing the work of coaches involved—and coordinating the project. The end result was positive, long-term change in behavior for the client executives—and a very positive experience for the coaches!

As my coaching clients know, our coaching involves a guarantee ... that the person being coached shows documented positive results through a mini-survey. The raters are not me, nor the coaching client, but instead the client's stakeholders. The mini-survey results of Marilyn's own coaching engagements also show documented positive results.

Though Marilyn's coaching has focused mainly on small business owners during her career, the exercises and concepts she presents in her book make sense for anyone who is taking charge of their own enterprise, their career, or finding their way through a personal challenge or transition. The 7 Steps she presents offer tools to improve anyone's personal management skills.

As I read through her book, it was interesting to learn more about her background, and what informs her coaching. Marilyn is an exceptional coach. She has a way of fitting into an environment and providing support and guidance in a manner that does not call attention to herself, but instead enhances the business owner's vision and personal style.

This book is being published during a time of global economic uncertainty. The topics are timely. Marilyn has brought together the wisdom of some of the greatest leadership thinkers in modern times, including several of my own mentors, and created a very readable resource book of tools which are especially vital in our changing environment.

Marilyn's book follows a principle I use in my work: A concept distilled into its simplest form saves everyone valuable time. Her book is small enough to carry around, yet carries the weight of great thinkers and concepts that not only make sense intellectually, but have also been proven to work. She has created a practical, useful tool full of helpful ideas which are balanced with practical how-to exercises and useful questions.

The tone of the book is friendly. It is like having Marilyn in the room. Give yourself ten minutes here, half an hour there, and read her book as an idea-generator for whatever issues you are facing. With wisdom distilled from her coaching practice, Marilyn's got it right. She clearly has her finger on the pulse of what you need to know today to manage yourself in a small business.

— **Marshall Goldsmith**

Marshall Goldsmith
New York Times, Wall Street Journal, BusinessWeek, USAToday and
Publisher's Weekly best-selling author of :

What Got You Here Won't Get You There (Hyperion)

MOJO: How to Get It, How to Keep It, and How to Get it Back When You Need It! (Hyperion)

Succession: Are You Ready? (Harvard Business Press)

The Organization of the Future 2 by Frances Hesselbein and Marshall Goldsmith (Jossey-Bass)

Leader of the Future 2 by Frances Hesselbein and Marshall Goldsmith (Jossey-Bass)

www.MarshallGoldsmithLibrary.com

A Personal Note

I have always been a creative sort. For me this means I live in a world of possibilities, which can often look like chaos to people who are not me.

In addition, I like quiet, neatness, simplicity, and order.

Finding balance has been easy for me, because I have an innate sense of order, and because I have unique skills of organization.

My goal in this book is to describe some of the tools I've used to bring order out of chaos, and to help you, the reader, create a foundation unique to your life that can serve as a platform of support, helping you live your own life confidently on your terms.

I want to acknowledge a special person who recently struggled through some very difficult times. It's still hard for me to look back on the years following an accident when I was not sure I would ever enjoy being around myself again, and whether I would ever again be capable of having a life of interest to me.

During those years I needed someone with the organizational skills I had before I got hurt, to help me navigate the myriad circumstances to weigh and decisions to make which could lead to recovery and meeting my own needs day to day, while also making reasonable sense to the people around me. This was a challenging feat, and I found that the time I was most vulnerable and needed the most support, was the time life called upon me to provide that support myself.

I didn't find anyone who could put heart and facts together the way I could before I got hurt, and I didn't find anyone who could help me navigate this overwhelming chaos the way I'd helped my clients before I got hurt. There was an unexpected lesson in this for me regarding the value of my skills.

During that time I wished so much that I had a guide to help me through. I honestly did not know if I'd ever be though, but I continued on as though I would. I found support from a previously uncovered deeper part of myself that knew I'd be okay and persistently guided me there, during a time I wasn't sure personally if I even wanted to be okay. The road was so hard. Getting hurt was easy. Recovering was the hard part.

I promised that precious, courageous Self-friend that if I ever got through those times I would put what I knew on paper so I could refer to it if I ever needed those skills again. I offer this also as my legacy to help others.

I learned to walk again after I got hurt by choosing to put in the tedious and painful effort required day after day instead of settling for life in a wheelchair. I'm becoming a public speaker and overcoming the conditioning of a rural Midwestern woman who was taught to be seen and not heard, and better yet, not to be noticed at all. I'm choosing to graciously live this precious life I have today by living as fully as possible while in balance with my current resources and abilities.

I present to you … me … just as I am. I welcome you … just as you are. I hope this book helps you live your own life with courage to reach more deeply inside yourself to express your authentic Self to the world.

I would love to hear from you along the way.

My very best wishes,
Marilyn McLeod
www.CoachMarilyn.com
San Diego 2010

How to Use This Book
ℰↃ

Quick Summary:

• This book is written to be as usable as possible. You can either:

• Read it sequentially
  • Just the "Quick Summary" and "Exercise" sections of each chapter, or ...
  • Continue reading for more depth.

• Look in the table of contents and follow a topic (xii).

• Choose a feeling or need from the Feelings and Needs charts. How does it fit what's going on for you, and for others you know (page 233)

• Kick back and read a few stories from Section Three (page 94)

Exercise:

1) Decide how you are going to use this book:

  • Reference book when you need new ideas
  • Study guide by yourself or with your coach
  • Improvement guide for your team, family, support group

2) Create time in your schedule to follow through with your intention above.

3) Is there anything in the way of you following through? If so, address this as best you can to support the improvement you want.

4) Send me an email occasionally to let me know how it's working for you! You will find the book website at http://www. CoachMarilyn.com.

ℰↄ

I won't mince words. This book is about courage. It's also about the tools I've found that have helped me get through the tough times. I will introduce you to some of my mentors whose friendship and wisdom have been a valuable component of my success thus far.

This experience we call life is not for the faint of heart. It takes courage to get up every day and face what cannot help on some level being unpredictable. Some people thrive on the adrenaline rush of the unexpected, enjoying the hunt. Other people create as routine and safe an existence as possible. We are all different people, and we each embody our own array of unknowns: our health, our mood, our choices.

I'm hoping you will become aware of the choices you have been making that affect your options much more than you know, and that you will take that awareness and make informed choices about situations and conditions that affect your life and the lives of those around you.

If from that conscious perspective you choose to live a life others (or even you) may have judged as ineffective or unflattering, I'll get in your corner and be your champion. I will trust you're making your best choice for the moment, and that as you see a better choice in the future, you will be ready to make another choice, or a series of other choices, either gradually or suddenly, as it makes sense for you.

The point is ... it comes from within you. My statements are only suggestions!! I won't tell you what to do, and I hope you don't let anyone else tell you what to do. It's your life. I hope you look within yourself to find your deeper truth, and make your own decisions.

I've written a reference book that I intend to use myself! Please take what works for you and discard the rest. Here's to courage as we share the journey together! I've organized this book so it can be used in a variety of ways:

Simple Efficiency
If you're in a hurry or you want the simple version, read the 'Quick Summary" of each chapter and do the exercises.

Food for Thought
In the next section of each chapter I share my thoughts and experiences and those of my mentors to help you broaden your thinking about how you might apply this concept in your own situation.

Stories
Read stories of several people who are in the process of building their future in the form of various enterprises and projects personal and professional.

Greater Depth
This book is intended to be an idea-generator, reference, and comfort food for the soul. I provide resources and urls in the book and on the website if you want to study any of these concepts in greater depth.

You can take this journey in several ways:

• Read the book and do the exercises by yourself.

• Ask a friend to read the book with you and do the exercises together.

• Start a group to study the material together and support each other as you try out the exercises.

• Visit the book website and join others who are reading the book, sharing your experiences and tracking your progress online. www.CoachMarilyn.com.

• I've included the complete bibliography online with easy links to help you find the materials.

Building a Future
Is it your birthday, or January 1st, or have you just had a major life change and you're thinking about what direction to take next? This book can help you sort out your options, and help you focus on a future plan.

As you're reading the book, I recommend:

• Take time to consider how these ideas and questions relate to you. Take as much time as you need. Start a journal and write down your impressions in phrases so you can remember later. Just take notes about your thoughts. They don't all have to make sense yet.

• If you feel you need more information to answer the questions, wander through the book either by looking up key words in the index at the back of the book, looking at the charts (page 233), or reading a story in Section Three (page 94).

• Change and transition can sometimes be lonely or daunting. Many people find that creating a routine in their lives helps them move forward. Most people seem to make more consistent progress toward their goals when they're accountable to someone besides themselves.

You'll find exercise worksheets in the back of this book (page 243).

Some Suggested Routines:

• Choose a time of day or a day of the week to read the book and do the exercises, and stick to your schedule.

• Are you hearing your friends or business associates making the same old negative comments over and over again? Are you looking for a positive environment that will help you trust in yourself and your future? Consider starting a study group, where everyone gets together once a week to discuss the section of the book they've read and applied between meetings.

• To create more accountability, ask someone you trust will be honest and fair with you to be your peer coach. Tell them what you plan to do and when, and schedule a regular time to check in with each other about the goals you set for yourselves. You can help each other stay on target. See Peer Coaching (page 180).

• You may be one of my coaching clients or a student in one of my courses. If so, please do the homework and let me know how things are going for you. I can only help you if you tell me what works and what doesn't.

I am always interested in learning new ideas! I'm sharing the best of what I've learned so far, and I expect you'll build on what you learn in the book. Let me know what you've discovered and invented as a result of being inspired by my book! It's like having grandchildren … I don't have to go through labor or pay for college … I just get to see traces of my labors of love reflected in your wonderful creations. That is my real payback … to see how you have used what I offer.

Backdrop

**"Whatever you can do, or dream you can, begin it.
Boldness has genius, power and magic in it."**

(attributed to Goethe)

CHAPTER 1:

Recession or Plenty

ℰℂ

Quick Summary:

• Fortunes, health and advantages come and go.

• Develop a range of strategies to respond to evolving conditions.

• Often the seeds of our solutions are in plain sight. It takes creative thought to uncover important assets we may have missed.

• To get out of a rut, it helps to understand areas of weakness honestly, and then to focus on where you want to go.

• Character wears well in any condition.

Exercise:

1) Make a list of your current reality: One list of what you like about your life and business now, and the other list of what you don't like.

2) Look honestly at both lists, and begin to create a vision of what you truly want that resonates deeply with the truth of who you are.

3) Step out of any mental constructs such as anger, judgment, criticism, diagnosis, blame and resentment. From that point of clarity, look at your 'don't like' list again. Are there people and resources on that list who could help you if you approached them in a positive, supportive way?

4) Write down any new perspective you now have about your own definition of recession and plenty.

శౖ

Let's start with the real reason you may have picked up this book: you have either just won the lottery, or the world economy is falling apart all around you, and you're wondering how you can possibly follow seven simple steps to success while you're feeling so very overwhelmed. I'll start with a story.

As I child we didn't have a television at home, so I spent my time watching and listening to the adults around me. I also paid attention to changes in the seasons, and watched how the trees and lawn outside my bedroom window would change during summer, autumn, winter and spring. I lived in the same house for many of my childhood years, so I could compare the size and position of the snowdrifts from year to year, and whether this fall the leaf colors would be brilliant and colorful, or whether the cold rain would turn them brown. I watched my own emotional responses through the long dreary months of winter, and then as spring teased and finally sprung with great gusto.

I learned by listening to adults that fortunes, health and advantages come and go. I heard stories of people's missteps both with prosperity and poverty. We all have our unique frame of reference about these issues. What I cared most about personally was my own values. I grew up very poor, and was worried about losing my values if I had money. I was relieved when I tested this out in adulthood to find I was still the same person, regardless of how much or how little was in my bank account.

How about you? Are you worried about making the right choices with some new advantage or windfall you've gained? Are you struggling to find a way to survive in a challenging environment?

It's a bit like the weather. Do you go into a panic when you see rain in the forecast, or it actually starts to rain? Maybe it's a full-on downpour or thunderstorm. Does your life change? Does this make it completely impossible to survive? If you are a farmer, it could change your fortune temporarily. Otherwise you can probably put on your raincoat or take your umbrella and continue on your way. Or you can wait until the rain has passed and then go on your errands.

Similarly, when the rain passes and you see blue skies and sunshine, do you become giddy breathing clean air and completely forget to go to work that day? Chances are you will remember your core commitments for the day and make some arrangements before you take a vacation day to sit in the park and watch the clouds go by.

The seven steps to success in this book will not solve your problems for you, or change the weather. What they can do is help you navigate your way through conditions while keeping what matters to you front and center. If you know what you want and don't want, and what your options are, you are much more likely to find favorable shelter or to attract unexpected opportunities to help you live your authentic values and best life.

Because most of my career has been working with small business owners, I began writing this book as a reference and handbook for my small business coaching clients. As I wrote, I had to acknowledge how closely our business and personal lives are, and that the principles I'm describing apply to any leader at any level, in any situation, either personally or in business.

In addition, to be completely fair, I had to acknowledge that the basic wisdom I'm drawing upon came from my own childhood experiences, so to give credit for courage and wisdom under duress, one of my stories is about myself as a ten year old child. I am writing a book that would have helped me improve my lot when I was young. If you are living under someone else's authority and have little room to maneuver to take care of your own needs, perhaps some of the ideas in this book will help you.

Because I've been aware from a young age that both wealth and poverty are transient, I have always valued the ability to be comfortable with either. As I've grown older, I've come to define wealth and poverty beyond the amount of money one has.

During the years I felt helpless while recovering from an injury, I looked back at my younger years without money and remembered wistfully how strong I was as I walked when I had no transportation, and gathered and prepared my own food when I had no food at home. The winters without heat challenged my survival skills, but I have not been able to match the beauty of my natural surroundings since leaving my childhood home. I had no money for clothes, so I learned to sew by practicing on hand-me-downs, creating my own clothes as I needed them. The resourcefulness that helped me survive childhood has helped me find creative solutions to challenges in my adult life.

I know people with all the advantages of supportive family, home, business, and health who spend their days feeling inadequate because of something they have not yet achieved, or overwhelmed and stressed with the responsibility of keeping what they've achieved.

In some ways wealth and poverty are a state of mind. In other ways they reflect how we use the resources we have. Sometimes it's about how we share and gain more, or how we set boundaries to take care of ourselves.

I return to my childhood wisdom: conditions change, so it's important to learn how to be comfortable with whatever shows up in our lives. In the meantime, it's important to do what we can to move closer to the life and career we want, and be flexible and creative in our thinking.

Are You Leaving Valuables on the Table?
Several years ago I visited the house where I was raised from age
ten to when I left home. It was a sunny summer day, many of
which I remember fondly from years past. The gravel driveway
providing access to our house from the main gravel road came
from the paved road which came from the city. Our private .8 mile
long driveway had long since grown over, and was now passable
only by walking.

I walked past the soybean fields and absentmindedly picked
a soybean pod as I had as a child, feeling a soft plant moving across
my hand as it brushed past several groups of leaves surrounding
the pod on the soybean plant, and then feeling the rough exterior
of the pod as I gently moved my fingers over the surface of the
soybean pod I'd picked.

I knew the cycle because I'd seen it over many years: As
the summer turned to fall, the rows of soybean plants in the fields
around the driveway and house would turn from green to gold,
and the pods from green to medium brown. If the pods were left
to their own devices, the pod would gradually open. The outside
skin of the pod would dry out and begin to curl, spilling the now
mature yellow soybean seeds onto the ground, ready to grow when
spring arrived. The farmers would be in the fields with their har-
vesting equipment just after the seeds had matured and the pods
were dry, and just before they opened and gave their seeds away.

Though I do have some positive memories (unending
beauty in myriad weather conditions of the rural landscape), I also
have grim memories (being so cold in the winter I couldn't close
my fingers tight enough to hold a piece of paper, so I had to invent
a way to turn the pages of a book without using fine dexterity).

My father was a staunch German who did not allow his
wife to work, and he usually drank the money that might have
gone for food or heat. I learned to live without money and to use
the resources and materials around me to create whatever I needed.

The drinking had its positive side: Dad was not aware enough to notice and undermine the inventive ways we found individually to survive our harsh environment.

Some kids keep a jar where they collect bugs or other caterpillars they can watch. I preferred to leave those where I found them in the wild, and just watch them in their native environment. My jar I watched as a kid contained soybeans.

I remember picking up that jar of soybeans many times over the five years I lived in that house. "There must be something valuable I could do with these soybeans," I always thought. But there was nothing in my culture or the books I read that gave me any clue. Soybeans were for farmers and livestock.

It was only many years later, as I was visiting my childhood home, walking down that long driveway, holding another soybean pod, that I made the connection. By then edamame was a popular food, and I'd learned about tofu and soy milk. My childhood intuition had been right as I had looked at my jar of soybeans. I had lived hungry, surrounded by fields of quality protein as far as I could see. I had just not taken the next step to turn the resource into what I needed.

Do you leave valuables on the table?

New resources and answers to our challenges are often hiding behind our limited view of the world around us.

Politics in the Workplace

Gary Ranker, a noted coach who specializes in Corporate Politics, helps his clients turn adversity into stepping stones.

> "Think about how difficult it would be to walk
> across a crowded room having just lost your vision.
> Without your sight, you bump into people, you
> have to ask if you are going in the right direction,
> and although you eventually get to the other side,

it is not at all as efficient as had you been able to see. You would have been able to clearly maneuver around the obstacles in the room and avoid any accidents or problems that could have gotten in your way.'

'Most people, when it comes to organizational politics, are politically "blind." They stumble through their political cultures and corporate environments, bumping into uncomfortable situations, stubbing their toes on bad gossip and rumors, and are cloaked by the sometimes spiteful agendas surrounding them. They feel lost in their business politics. Unfortunately, many business people in the corporate world are not aware of, or just cannot "see" the agendas of others around them.'

'They don't know if other peoples' agendas are an obstacle, or perhaps a source of assistance, to the navigation of their own corporate worlds. Other peoples' agendas are like wind on the ocean for a sail boat. Sometimes the wind fills your sails and helps you, and sometimes it blows you off course. But even those peoples' agendas that are blowing against you can still be useful if you know how to jibe and tack. Good sailors can use the wind to go in any direction. In the same manner it is possible to learn to more effectively jibe and tack through corporate politics to attain one's goals.'

'Although we may be blind to these agendas, we can still develop a way to "feel" our way around them.

Think of it as having extra antennae that pick up or sense these social and political agendas. When we have these social antennae, we can better sense these agendas to use to our advantage.'

'With the right coaching, guidance, and insight, we can learn to grow and develop our own social and political antenna, to help us navigate the corporate worlds around us."

Gary Ranker
Corporate Politics Coach
Political Dilemmas at Work
www.GaryRanker.com

Another Perspective

My friend Matthew Stillman has another way of looking at this:

The principle to work with is - if you think you lack something...give it.

If you think you lack money - give your wealth.
If you are hungry - give nourishment

If you need sleep - give rest to someone.
If you lack friends - give friendship.
If you lack love, give that.

Look at it this way ... giving your wealth isn't giving your money. Ask yourself the question ... what is your wealth?

Matthew Stillman

Matthew is currently wearing several hats, including documentary filmmaker, former Food Network program developer, improv actor, husband, and construction foreman for a remodel in his family's home. At this point he's one of many laid off from his day job, and simply identifies as 'ninja'.

The Other Woman

I'd been dating David for several months, when suddenly I had a feeling something had changed between us. Whenever I asked him about this, he told me it was my problem. But things just didn't feel right. I felt a painful gap in our connection. I was frustrated with conflicting messages and there didn't seem to be anything I could do to get to the truth.

I happened to know the woman he was involved with before me, and I had respect for her, so I bravely gave Annette a call with an open heart. She was wonderful. She told me the two of them had gotten back together. Then she asked me how I was. She was sincerely interested in my wellbeing, and kept asking and being attentive to my feelings and needs until I felt supported and connected again.

I ended up feeling betrayed by the man who professed to care so much about me, and totally supported by the 'other woman'. Who would I choose to be my friend in the future? The one who told me the truth and then was there to help me heal.

I'm not saying that approaching the 'other woman' with an open heart will always end up being a positive experience. I am saying that I learned not to assume someone was my enemy.

I learned that hearing the truth honestly allowed me to stay connected, and that being treated with respect and being included in the conversation were more important to me than getting my way. The truth allowed me to honestly understand the landscape I was in, so I had more power to chart a meaningful future course of my own.

Which is recession and which is plenty? Sometimes it's difficult to tell, when you take a larger view.

CHAPTER 2

Success

ॐ

Quick Summary:

• Everyone has their own definition of success and their own reasons for being in business.

• For better or worse, we often impose our own definitions on other people.

• Sometimes finding our authentic path to success and happiness involves being willing to look at new ideas, and try new things.

• Getting past the stigma of being wrong has immense benefits.

Exercise:

1) Write down your own definition of success. Now think of someone who loves you unconditionally, without regard to your material or social success. From their perspective, read the definition you've just written down. Does it ring true as your own?

2) Do an experiment to find out more about yourself. Think about something you have strong feelings about, and then ask some people for their ideas about this topic. Watch how you respond. Do you notice yourself reaching for a pen to write down the new ideas you're learning, or do you hear yourself defending your deeply held convictions?

3) If you heard yourself talking defensively, stop and notice what you are saying to yourself right now. Are you berating yourself for doing something wrong, or are you giggling in loving amusement because you caught yourself doing something silly again?

ℰↄ

If I ask you to define success, what comes to mind first? Financial security, luxurious lifestyle, loving relationships, power, robust health, spiritual connection, achievement of a lifetime goal or cause? We all define success in our own way, and what we call success at one point in our lives can evolve into something completely different at another point. We may discover halfway through our lives that what we are calling success is really someone else's definition and not ours at all!

My definition of success for myself: Am I happy? Growing up as I did with Garrison Keilor in rural Lake Wobegon, Minnesota, dutifully becoming the strong woman admired by Our Lady of Perpetual Responsibility, it took me several years to begin to understand the concept of 'happiness', and even longer to make the great leap to giving myself permission have some.

It's not so easy for me to notice from outward appearances whether someone else is happy. My definition of success for the people around me: Are they trying instead of whining? I'm happier when I'm around people who take responsibility for themselves and contribute something useful to the world around them.

Consider the Possibility
Several years ago a new neighbor moved in next door and we became friends. As we became acquainted Melodey shared her plans to find a job. A few weeks later she mentioned it again, this time with a sigh, and a confession that she actually dreaded finding

another job. She listed the kinds of jobs she thought she could land, and told me how depressed she felt every time she thought about how much she would not enjoy the successful outcome of her job search.

By that time I'd noticed several of Melodey's skills that I thought could be marketable as an entrepreneur. I remember clearly the moment she later told me had been a turning point in her life.

I looked at her, paused, and asked, "Can you consider the possibility that you might be able to earn a living without getting another job?"

She paused as well and took in this new idea. She spent the next few weeks planning her new business-building project, and began a consistent process of marketing and delivery of her chosen products and services. It's been ten years, and she now has a successful business as an independent musician, creating music on her terms.

Her response to reading this story: "Yes, it was a pivotal moment in my life and I will be forever grateful to you for the message you gave me that day. Venturing into the unknown is terrifying and empowering and I thank you for giving me the verbal "push!"."

You may not want to be an entrepreneur or a musician! I'm betting there *is* something you would like to improve about your life that you feel discouraged about implementing, and my core message to you is … "Can you consider the possibility that something wonderful and beyond your current frame of reference is actually more achievable than it appears to you right now?"

I'm a coach by profession. I help people find ways to help themselves. Hidden in this lofty mission is the reality that improvement means change. The word 'change' has been noted to induce a stress response in people! I find that different people have a whole variety of responses to the opportunity to change the course of their lives, to improve their health, to change habits to support greater happiness.

I know Alan and Steve who light up and are completely present, listening with full interest when a new idea is presented. And I know Joe and Sam whose first response is some form of 'no'. Guess which men are more successful? You guessed it ... the men who embrace change.

I didn't start out my life embracing change. My father assured us he had never made a mistake, and had all the answers. The joke in our family was that he was never a little boy (because that would make him ... even at some distant point in his life ... as vulnerable and fallible as we were as children). I grew up taking the advice I once read in a book, "It is better to keep one's mouth shut and be thought a fool than to open it and remove all doubt".

I was afraid to be wrong.

Why it was so scary to be wrong I can't say, because now that I'm more interested in what's true than who's right, I can't even remember why I spent so much energy protecting myself. And it ran my life for so many years! I count my blessings that I was able to change that habit. Life is so much more fun this way!

How did I make the leap from being closed to new ideas to embracing an open conversation to discover new ideas? I met a man who didn't mind being wrong. He was a great role model for me, never judging me as I was judging myself. Gradually I was able to feel safe, and stop the negative criticism of myself and others.

Success in Business

Even the definition of success in business varies by individual. One obvious reason to go into business is to make a profit, to sustain your chosen lifestyle.

Some people start a business even though they don't need the money. They may enjoy the process of creating money, or creating a successful venture, or leading people. They may be bored at home and want somewhere to go every day. They may enjoy the social aspect of their business, whether or not they turn a profit.

They may believe in a cause, and see their venture as a way to make a difference. They may have inherited a "successful" role or position they're not sure what to do with.

Back to my personal definition of success, "Am I happy?" Whatever your reason for being in business, it's easier to make successful decisions for yourself when you are conscious of the reasons you want to be in your business.

CHAPTER 3

Ownership

ஐ

Quick Summary:

• Ownership is a multifaceted concept.

• Ownership in a small business means wearing many hats, including boss and employee.

• We are better equipped to run our own business when we take responsibility for our own decisions, and management of our own resources.

• Blame and excuses are expensive.

• Self-motivation, self-responsibility and clear, objective vision are like gold.

• When considering taking on a partnership, consider carefully, and then think it over again.

Exercise:

1) Think about yourself and your reasons for wanting to be in business. Write down your thoughts.

2) Think about who you want to share ownership with, and why. Write down what you expect each owner to contribute, and what you think the business owes them. Beyond the money, are there intangibles involved?

3) Think about the functions you expect your enterprise will require to run. Which functions are supplied by an owner, and which will you hire out? Try to clarify everything. (Your ideas may evolve as you read the 7 Steps in this book.)

4) Look at the list of people you plan to involve in your enterprise. How much do you really trust them? Have they demonstrated integrity and dependability in the past? In what ways can you not count on them?

5) Now look at yourself and apply the same standards to yourself. Can you really count on yourself to carry out your part of this business? Make a list of improvements you would like to see in yourself and everyone else involved before you move forward.

෨

This chapter discusses the initial concept I had in mind when I began writing this book, and it is now the last chapter I'm writing. Nathaniel Branden told me he sometimes writes a book because he wants to learn more about a topic himself. Perhaps that is the path I've taken with this book without realizing it.

I've noticed for a long time that I have an unusual perspective, because my personal experience of history spans much more than one lifetime of change in our society. When I read Paul Hersey's book about his father's life, I identified with the way his father grew up, because the pioneer-like conditions so closely resembled my own experience as a child. Many of my closest friends are in their 80s, or my parent's age. When I was in my teens and I went home with friends from school, I spent as much time with my friend's parents talking about adult issues as I did with my friends talking about children's issues. Though initially I spent years actually being afraid of computers, my current technical expertise with the Internet makes me a contemporary of the youngest techies who grew up with technology as their first language.

There is another aspect of this historical span that I've had a more difficult time putting words to. It is a very clear concept to me, and I've spent the past year going to many people who I think will see it more clearly than I, but so far no one has been able to help me find the words. Frances Hesselbein told me, "The words will come." Tomorrow my book manuscript is due, so let's see if the words come now.

I think this concept has something to do with the differences between Daniel Boone and the millenials entering the workforce in the 2000s. I like many characteristics of the millenials: they are talented, sociable, optimistic, educated, open-minded, able to influence, collaborative and achievement-oriented. I sometimes wish I had their gumption to expect my employer to bend the needs of the company to my private vacation or exercise plans. More than that, even though they are much more involved in the world than I was at their age, I worry about their ability to handle the responsibilities of running a world that requires the skills and fortitude of someone like Daniel Boone. Actually, I've had this growing concern for several decades.

This theory began when I was young, when I heard stories about how some of the early businessmen in a young United States built infrastructure, department store chains, and other large and prosperous companies. Often the story went, "The man worked hard and built a company. The woman had children and went shopping. The children grew up and didn't do much with their lives, and were unable to take over the family business." I had a suspicion that the further removed from what creates greatness each new generation became, the less empowered we as a society were becoming.

By the way, I know some of the younger generations have carried on fine leadership legacies in their companies, so I do not mean to make a blanket statement here. I just noticed an interesting trend.

A related social observation also aroused my curiosity. Please know that I am not putting forth my childhood experience as something to emulate. I'm just asking the question … is there something to learn from this? I grew up thinking the easiest work in the world was to raise children, because you just laid in bed (my Mom) or went away for a week or so (my Dad) and let them raise themselves. I never questioned this until I was in my 40s (luckily my intuition told me during my child-bearing years that I wasn't prepared to have children!) and a young mother told me, "Oh, you have to watch children every second." Surprised, I asked, "Why?!" She looked at me in surprise and said, "Well, they could put something in their mouth and swallow it, or do any number of things to hurt themselves!"

Many times I've asked myself how I survived childhood, and this was one more time. I admit I've heard of several children who have perished at a young age in spite of attentive parents and advantageous circumstances. At that moment I wondered, "How in the world did my parents stay drunk and in bed during our growing-up years, have too much pride to apply for food stamps until we were all safely grown and gone, and have all four children make it to adulthood?!" I do know one factor is that I was not prepared to accept the results of their neglect, and I took responsibility for my own survival. The rest is a mystery.

The reason I'm putting this into the "Ownership" chapter is I think the answer has something to do with how we approach our work, and whether or not we are ready to be successful in our own business. The individualism of Daniel Boone led him to take responsibility for his own actions and forge his own destiny. In a frontier environment, the only other choice was to perish. This attitude was the foundation of America's entrepreneurial success.

I asked Nathaniel Branden what happens when the millennial culture meets the frontier of a world economic collapse, and there is no more excess prosperity to support the lifestyle they've become accustomed to. They might suddenly find they have to be responsible. They've never had to think like that before. Would they pout and feel put upon? He responded, "Some of them would lash out and pout, feel the world is not delivering to them what it owes them, and somebody's got to fix something. It would be the lone individual who comes up with some idea that might be in the direction of a solution."

Who owns your business? If you're creating your own business from scratch, hopefully that is you. If you have gone into debt to open your new business, maybe it's the bank. If you have a partner, you may each think you own the business, but be ready to blame the other person when something goes wrong, or if the business requires something that inconveniences you.

My point is … your business *will* inconvenience you. It *will* be challenging. When you are a sole proprietor, you are wearing all of the hats, and the buck stops with you. It's hard to blame someone when you look around and you are the only one there.

The other side of the coin is … having your own business gives you complete freedom to make whatever choices make sense to you. Yes, depending on your industry there are regulations to follow, there are customers to satisfy, there are cash constraints and logistical considerations, but if you don't like the way things are going, you can change direction. You can cultivate a new target customer base, drop a product line, change the way you do business, or give up on this one and start a new business completely.

There isn't much security. There will be times of plenty, when so much work comes in you can't keep up with it, and there will be times you can't bring in a new customer no matter what you do. What you do with your resources when they are flowing freely will affect if you are able to weather the leaner times. After a few years, you will probably discover specific times of year that things slow down naturally, and you can plan vacations or catch-up projects during that time. I usually do my taxes in December, and take a vacation in July.

How much of your business ownership are you sharing with others? If this is a family business, you may be sharing everything. If this is a partnership, there is one or more other person you are sharing with based on your agreements.

Before you actually take on a partner, I'd like you to ask yourself … is this someone you would marry? Do you trust them enough? Are they true to their word? Will they follow through? Do you want a long term relationship with them where you are vulnerable to their foibles as well as what they can contribute to the business? What will you do if things don't work out?

I know some partnerships that work beautifully. I know many more that have pulled marriages and friendships apart, and caused businesses to fail.

One option is to maintain your own independent business entity, have a network of other professionals you trust who own their own businesses, and share referrals with each other. This makes it less costly to bring in someone with new expertise as you need it, and easier to refer based on dependability and demonstrated good results. You might be able to share the cost of supplies or services that you all need, and benefit informally without having to own each other's businesses.

A book that sheds light on the concepts of autonomy and self-reliance:

Taking Responsibility by Nathaniel Branden
Simon & Schuster
ISBN 0-684-83248-8

♫

"I started my business 25 years ago. That's a quarter of a century already! I'm not getting rich, but I don't have to worry about being fired. If I downsize, I'm the last one to go!"

Neil Sturman
Physical Therapist
Encinitas, California

CHAPTER 4

Image

୨୨

Quick Summary:

• The image that really sells has less to do with the cost and flashiness of your promotional materials, and more to do with:

> • The depth of personal authenticity you convey, and
> • How much you sincerely care about the other person's wellbeing.

• To convey mastery of your business message: practice, practice, practice.

• Sincere appreciation of others can be the most powerful incentive program.

Exercise:

1) Can you convey your message effectively without PowerPoint?

2) The next time you're in front of a prospective customer or stakeholder, notice how you're coming across:

> • Do you push your 30 second commercial at them whether they want it or not? When you do this, how often does this lead to a new customer?

• Do you listen first to understand who you are talking to and what they need? When you do this, how often does this lead to a follow up conversation?

3) Ask people around you (who will tell you the truth) how often you let them win, and whether they consider you a good listener.

4) Think about your presentation from your ideal customer's point of view. What about image would turn them on, and what would turn them off?

℘

How important is image to you? My natural style is to prefer function over form, and I have only invested time, attention and resources into my image because I notice how much outward appearances affect first impressions. What else do people have to go on before they've had a chance to know and trust me over time?

The way a person is perceived has something to do with neatness, promptness, and courtesy. It also has to do with inner confidence and posture. Cringing does not inspire customers to buy, and neither does grandiosity. Authenticity communicates most powerfully.

Do you know how you are seen? If you can watch the people around you as they respond to you, you can learn more than you might expect. My first experience with this was as a young member of a corporate team. I was invited to a meeting, and charged with taking notes on the white board.

I'd done my homework and read some books about how to make a presentation. I was dutifully standing with my arms at my side, hands clasped together in front. (Since I've worked with Arthur Joseph, I now know this as the 'fig leaf' position … not the most powerful!)

In any case, I was following all of the rules, ready to write the next point on the white board, when I noticed two young men in the back row pointing at me and having a grand old time laughing. It took me a few moments to realize I was holding the marker in a very perky way in my clasped hands in front of me!

Well, I can say I've successfully remembered to avoid that ever since! Luckily I always smile as I remember. Feeling ashamed is just debilitating and doesn't do anyone any good. I simply allow myself to learn.

Another question: Can people tell what you're thinking, even if you don't say the words? I thought I was safe with my judgments and disdain until a more mature co-worker informed me that it didn't matter whether I said the words or not; I was communicating the message loud and clear. As I've paid attention over time, I can certainly see how true that is. Again, cultivating authenticity is valuable ... even going so far as to give up on the judgment and disdain and have true respect and warm regard for each human being I'm privileged to meet, even if I don't like what they do or what they are saying.

I've learned something very interesting from Arthur Joseph that goes beyond how I hold the marker when I'm in front of an audience. It has to do with what I hide from the world as a matter of course.

Arthur Samuel Joseph, vocal coach to top performers and leaders, encourages his clients to believe in their Self. According to Arthur, the secrets we try to hide from the world are only amplified in our voice and how we present ourselves, and we are much more powerful when we live authentically from the core of who we really are.

I asked Arthur to describe what he meant by the "Self". He said,

> "The deeper Self is who I am. It is connected to the Voice, the inner voice. I coach my clients to always be conscious of Self, though not self conscious. It is a very intimate part of us. I strive to always stay present within my Self to the best of my ability, which I achieve largely through deeper listening.'

> 'I speak about the journey always going inward toward discovery of the deeper Self, and never outward toward accomplishment and achievement of goals.'

> 'How do I get to deeper listening? Sometimes I begin with conscious loving breath, because that is my connection, coming and going from one plane to the other, staying in contact with my spiritual self while living out here in this finite plane.'

> 'Simply allowing a conscious loving breath is the connector.'

> 'The Self is also the state of being that I strive to always reside in. It is a very present, a very conscious place, but not based on egotism. It is not all about me. It is based in recognition and allowance that it is alright to claim my Self. I do not have to ask permission. I do not have to worry about what you might think of me being this Self.'

'But at the same time, it is not about the egotistical aspect of that, but the embodiment of it from a mind body spirit construct."

Arthur Samuel Joseph
Vocal Strategist and Coach
Creator of Vocal Awareness System™
Vocal Power
Voice of a Leader
www.VocalAwareness.com

What is the purpose of the image you are presenting to potential customers and stakeholders? I'm going to assume you would like to be taken seriously, and you would like people to respect and trust you.

• Think about how you would like to be treated. Would your customers like you to treat them that way?

• Look over Marshall Goldsmith's twenty annoying habits (page 154). Do you see yourself in any of them?

• Think about the values and messages that build lasting relationships.

For instance, what does it cost to give appreciation? Gary Ranker was named by Forbes as one of the top five coaches. He works primarily with traders on Wall Street, where consideration for the feelings of others probably is not one of the top values held by many of those who work to stay afloat in that fast-moving environment. He has an interesting reflection about appreciation and profit. He says he often tells clients that giving appreciation costs nothing, and increases money.

You have the most powerful resource ever invented very close to you … your own ability to choose how you think, how you feel, and what you do.

You may feel shy about stepping up to be all you can be. I know this place; I've been there several times. I always marvel at how comfortable I become after making what seems like a huge leap to a new improvement in my image, which of course challenges my current self concept. I find in a short while the new 'me' soon becomes a natural part of who I am, and I'm ready for the next improvement!

If you're shedding old conditioning and moving closer to your authentic Self, then improving your image can become almost easy and even fun!

♫

"Be so good they can't ignore you."

Steve Martin
Comedian, Muscian, Actor

CHAPTER 5

Legacy

ઝ

Quick Summary:

• Thinking about the legacy we want to leave helps us balance short-term thinking with what lasts.

• Getting beyond the paradigms of winners and losers, who belongs and who are the outsiders, and who is right and wrong, helps us bridge current challenges to paradigms that work cross-culturally and over longer periods of time.

• What we do each day and how we live our lives may be more powerful than any legacy planning.

• Part of being successful is giving back.

Exercise:

1) Try Marshall Goldsmith's exercise: 95 year old man or woman (page 156).

2) Think about what matters to you and your customers and stakeholders. Is there a contribution you can make to your local community to address a need in this area?

3) Think about where you came from, and how people still in that situation may be struggling. Is there something you can do to make life easier for them, or to help them succeed?

4) Think about what you've learned during your life and career. Is there something you can package and turn into a gift or product that could help others?

℟

Legacy connotes wisdom to me. Something that takes time to develop, that will last and bring value to posterity. I expect you would prefer to leave a legacy that is appreciated after you are long gone, instead of being remembered as someone who created a mess for others to clean up.

The concept of legacy helps me think beyond my current situation. Realistically, it's difficult to know how what I create today will be viewed by generations after me, or even how I will view it at a different stage in my own life. All I can do is live my life and create my projects in line with my values, taking into consideration how what I'm doing affects others, and how it might affect future generations.

Have you created something in your life that you would like to last beyond your lifetime, or beyond your current occupation's prime performance period?

Have you grown beyond what might seem like insurmountable challenges, and have you learned something you can pass along to others? Can you turn what you have learned into a gift for people still struggling? Can you mentor someone who wants to take a similar path to your own?

Do you see a problem in the world that you have a solution for? Do you have the resources to offer the solution, or can you find the resources and backing to do so? Would it be even more helpful to initiate a dialog with the people who have the need, to see if your solution matches their culture, and if not, if there's a way to modify your solution to the reality of their day to day life?

Are you part of a group that is challenged, and you notice there's a culture of despair instead of finding solutions? Maybe you can be the voice of hope. Maybe you can begin to look for ways to improve the situation. Maybe you can read a book, or start talking to people, or look at available resources in a new way. Maybe you can notice someone with a need, and someone else with a resource, and introduce them to each other.

ℰℴ

Sometimes we are not even aware of our own gifts to others. Ms. Violet Panzram was my fourth grade teacher, which means I was ten years old in her class. She was probably considered the nerd of teachers by her peers at school. When we were walking in a line through the hallway and we passed another class, she would call out to them, "Hurray for books!" Her classroom was filled with books. On every wall there were bookshelves floor to ceiling, all filled with different kinds of books. She loved books. She would schedule a quiet hour every single day for us to sit at our desks and read a book. We could borrow one book at a time from the bookshelves, and leave it in our desk when we were not reading it.

When she said 'quiet time', she meant it! Occasionally when we were quietly reading, one student would forget he or she was supposed to ask permission before standing up and walking around, and suddenly Ms. Panzram would say, "Alright, everyone, stand up and walk around! See, that is what happens when you don't ask permission. It's chaos." We would all get a little exercise and then sit down quietly to read our books again.

That year in school was significant for me. I was old enough to really begin being conscious of the problems at home, and the heavy responsibilities I was carrying for the mess I didn't create. I needed a friend, and Ms. Panzram was always interested in me and what I was thinking. I felt special when she let me borrow the teacher's edition workbook for the Spanish class we watched weekly on television. She told me I was the only student in the class who was interested in learning Spanish. It was true. And I was very interested. I studied the Spanish workbook at home until I'd learned everything in the book. I read books about linguistics at the local public library. I went on to study German, French, and Russian in high school, and Spanish, Vietnamese and others in college. I've made friends from all over the world, sharing our lives between our cultures.

Occasionally I would stop by Ms. Panzram's classroom to visit her after I graduated from fourth grade. I continued this until I ran away from home during the fall semester of my senior year of high school, when living life on my own really became front and center, and I didn't see her for some time. I read a funeral notice in the newspaper one day for my third grade teacher, and decided to attend. There was Vi, and we became fast friends. Tearfully, I began to tell her what a difference she had made in my life when I was ten, and in my future thus far. She would have none of that. She was a Quaker and not at all interested in self-aggrandizement. She was not great in any sense of the word, she said, "I was just living my life."

She made a difference to me, just living her life.

≈

I've been very lucky to have such wonderful teachers. Truthfully, sometimes my teachers were not as helpful, though sometimes they tried to be … like my third grade teacher. She would chide me for having chapped and bleeding hands when I came to school in winter, and tell me I should take better care of myself. I honestly was doing the best I could under the circumstances, and the smelly, greasy lotion she made me rub into my hands didn't seem to help much. But she meant well.

Most of my teachers have helped me take one more step out of my original circumstances, moving somewhere closer to a life that better matches the best of me and who I am authentically. And I sincerely thank each one of them! What I offer back to the world is my legacy, and also theirs.

The point is also that I've been willing to learn. Who do you know that is willing to learn?

ℂ

I'm going to tell a story that is difficult for me to share. I'm telling the story because to me it illustrates what can happen when we don't look beyond ourselves when we are choosing a strategy to deal with other people. When I'm tempted to push someone harder who I know is already suffering, I remember this story and step back to see if there is another approach I might choose instead.

As a teenager I worked for Head Start. Head Start is a wonderful program. At that time 90% of the children enrolled were living in families where income was below poverty level. The program was designed to prepare disadvantaged children for kindergarten, and help families improve their quality of life. The tone of the program was very inclusive and supportive.

As a teenager, I also began to have a social life. A young man I dated a few times during that period worked in a collection agency. When we met at the end of one day for dinner, he told me about his day. He was proud of how he had handled a tough collection client, thoroughly insulting him. I was uncomfortable hearing this, and we began drifting apart. He was young then and perhaps has reconsidered his strategy since. While his victory felt good in the short term, the effects didn't help his agency collect the money he was after. I don't know what the rest of his client's day was like, but I did hear that night the man he had pushed so hard during the day went home and beat his wife to death. Their daughter, one of our Head Start children, was home.

℘

Violence comes in many forms. Just because you win in one way does not mean you win in another way. Before you take an action that affects another person, try to think whether you would be proud to have the important people in your life watching, and whether coming from compassion might get you further than a show of force.

How do you want the world to remember you?

What can you do today to make this world a better place?

You can actually start right where you are, and how you are living your life. Ask Marshall Goldsmith's question: What can I do to be a better husband/wife/son/daughter/co-worker/friend?

Ask yourself if you are expressing in your day to day life who you really are. Are you sharing your gifts with the world as you live day to day?

If so, you never know who might be watching, and whose life you may change without ever knowing.

Succession Planning

I've seen a whole range of succession implementation, from the CEO showing up one day to find out they've been replaced, to the CEO holding onto their role until their death finally keeps them from reporting to the office! I do not say which is right or wrong; I simply have suggestions for you as the leader.

Even in a small business, succession planning is important. Depending on the size and legal structure of your small business, you may or may not have the authority to choose your successor. It still makes sense to plan for contingencies, assuming you care about the future of your organization beyond your own tenure.

Frances Hesselbein says you should begin planning for when and how you will leave your position the day you begin the new job. She also says your last year in the position should be the most exuberant year of your whole career. You plan it this way.

Marshall Goldsmith, in his book *Succession: Are You Ready?* explores this topic. After coaching over 100 top CEO's, Marshall says that almost no occupational group is more personally identified with their jobs than CEO's. After a while, this is not just what you do – it becomes a very large part of who you are. At the CEO level – the handoff is far from impersonal – it is extremely personal!

The process Marshall outlines in his book:

• Slowing down, and making peace with slowing down
• Letting go and moving on to create a 'great rest of your life!'
• Choosing who to develop as your successor
• Evaluating internal coaching candidates
• Coaching your successor
• Involving key stakeholders
• Becoming a CEO coach-facilitator
• Passing the baton

For more information:
Succession: Are You Ready? by Marshall Goldsmith
Harvard Business School Press
ISBN 978-1422118238

Social Sector
One of my first positions as an employee was with the Office of Economic Opportunity in rural Minnesota where I learned about helping people help themselves rather than giving a handout. As I supported the people delivering training and assistance to the poor,

I was in a curious position of learning as well as helping. I also began to realize my own position socially, as most of the families we helped were in better circumstances than my own.

As I grew older and became more familiar with the organization, I was given more responsibilities, this time with their Head Start program. I was impressed with the design of the program. At the time we had four components: Health, Education, Parent Involvement, and Social Services. Each of the coordinator positions and most of the teacher aid positions were held by parents. The tone of the entire program was a holistic approach to helping an entire community, with everyone learning and contributing as they were able.

My next positions were in the corporate world, and from there I began my own small business, where I've been ever since. I've thought about the social sector often, and only recently have considered the possibility of becoming involved there again. The more time I spend with Frances Hesselbein, the more I'm motivated to find ways I can contribute.

Social sector organizations noted by Jim Collins, author of Good to Great include: education, healthcare, churches, the arts, social services, cause-driven nonprofits, police, government agencies, and military units.

Jim Collins wrote a special monograph as a companion to *Good to Great*, where he states, "I have come to see that it is simply not good enough to focus solely on having a great business sector. If we only have great companies, we will merely have a prosperous society, not a great one. Economic growth and power are the means, not the definition, of a great nation."

He suggests adopting a 'language of greatness' which applies to both business and social sectors. In his monograph he discusses questions that social sector leaders face which are different from the business sector:

• Defining 'great' without business metrics
• Getting things done within a diffuse power structure
• Getting the right people on the bus within social sector constraints
• Rethinking the economic engine without a profit motive
• Building momentum by building the brand

Frances Hesselbein is often honored for her role in developing the discipline of leadership. What is she saying in 2009 about leadership? First she quotes Peter Drucker when he said before 2000, "'The next decade will be a decade of great political turmoil in many parts of the world, including the United States.' At that time people said, 'What is wrong with Peter, why is he so pessimistic?' He was not pessimistic. He was prescient and he was very sober about the coming ten years. It had not yet happened. Peter said, 'I never predict. I simply look out the window and see what is visible but is not yet seen. It is already there, visible, but not yet seen.'"

Again she quotes Peter Drucker: "'It is not business, it is not government, it is the social sector that may yet save the society.' Peter was very sober about the direction we were going, and it is as though he did predict even though he said he never predicts. Look at what has happened in that ten year period, we are nine years through. It is not business, it is not government, it is the social sector that may yet save our society."

Frances goes on to talk about how essential our democracy is, and then presents the current plight of our schools, saying in New York City one of two children will not graduate from high school, one out of five in Los Angeles, and she laments the 5.5 million young people ages 16-24 who live on the streets of our cities, jobless, homeless, hopeless, no future.

"I think there have been two institutions that have sustained the democracy since the beginning of our country. One is the U.S. Army and the other is public education. We are stretching one, and public education is failing millions of our children. Both are essential. You cannot sustain a democracy unless you educate all of your children. For too many people these are the invisible children. They are not. What happens to a country when we do not educate all of our children? So far our response has been to build more prisons. That is not what a democracy does."

She quotes one of her mentors, John W. Gardner: "This nation could die of comfortable indifference to the problems that only citizens can solve."

Frances is currently working with a local faith-based organization that urges each church to adopt a school, and make sure it has a library, textbooks, materials, computers and opportunities for the teachers.

Frances leaves me with this mission: "I have a sense of urgency. We need to take care of our children, and we need to improve the level of trust in our country. We have the highest level of cynicism and the lowest level of trust in my whole lifetime, in my own country. What can we do individually and in groups to build a higher level of trust?" Frances believes in circular leadership, which means she trusts us to be the citizens in our communities to reach out and improve our society. "All of us have a responsibility," she says. "It is not someone else's business. It is our business."

For more information:

Leader to Leader
www.LeadertoLeader.org

The Five Most Important Questions You Will Ever Ask About Your Organization by Peter F. Drucker with Jim Collins, Philip Kotler, James Kouzes, Judith Rodin, V. Kasturi Rangan, and Frances Hesselbein
Leader to Leader Institute
ISBN 978-0470227565

Good to Great and the Social Sectors by Jim Collins
Collins Business
ISBN 978-0-9773264-0-2

Good to Great by Jim Collins
HarperCollins
ISBN 0-06-662099-6

Hesselbein On Leadership by Frances Hesselbein
Jossey-Bass
ISBN 978-0787963927

On Leadership by John W. Gardner
Free Press
ISBN 978-0029113127

7 Steps to Success

YOU • CUSTOMERS • BUSINESS • FOCUS • SALES • FOLLOW-UP • REVIEW

The 7 Steps

This section is about starting a new small business, or becoming more successful in your small business. The principles can be applied to other projects and situations; I will let you decide what fits and what does not. I've included some stories that illustrate various points of view.

If you're thinking of starting a new business of your own, you may think first of the skills you have that could be marketable. That is an important consideration, but it's not where I start. You can't just quit and walk away from your own business as easily as you can quit and walk away from a job. If you're going to create a role for yourself that you'll be living with day in and day out because you own the business, then I think it's highly valuable to create something you will enjoy doing day in and day out for years!

So I start with **YOU**:

Step 1:   **You**
Step 2:   **Customers**
Step 3:   **Business**
Step 4:   **Focus**
Step 5:   **Sales**
Step 6:   **Follow-up & Delivery**
Step 7:   **Review & Celebrate**

CHAPTER 6

You

ಙ

Quick Summary:

• Who runs your engine? As a small business owner, you are the most valuable resource your business has. Without you, nothing in your business happens.

• Your health and happiness are a primary consideration in the long term success of your venture.

• Creating a life close to your values helps your happiness level.

Exercise:

1) Think about you and what really makes you happy. Write down specifics that come to mind.

2) Think about times you feel stifled, discouraged, uncomfortable. Write down the situations that stimulate this feeling, and what specifically you don't like about it.

3) Think about yourself and all that you are. What aspects of yourself that make you happy remain untapped?

4) If you could have an ideal day, an ideal job, an ideal customer, an ideal life, what would it be like? Dream, and take notes!!!

STEP 1: IT IS ABOUT YOU

STEP 1: IT IS ABOUT YOU

Accept that you are the one who must champion your new creation.

You may think your product or service is your starting point, but your key is closer to home. You are the one who will be putting in the long hours to bring your vision to fruition. You have to be healthy to carry this responsibility, and you have to be happy to carry it long enough to make it work.

What makes you happy? What do you especially enjoy doing, and who do you most like to spend time with? What are your values? What roles most appeal to you? Define a role, career, product or company that matches who you are authentically as closely as possible.

Your Business Engine

What is the most important factor to your success as a sole proprietor, and how can you take very good care of this factor?

Think back to a time you felt really 'on'. Was it a situation where you were in charge, knowing just what to do, directing people and resources effectively to the right places, and the situation resolved smoothly into a positive result? Was it a time your fans listened adoringly as you explained the key concepts of your new project? Think of the situation, and look at which of your needs were getting met during this experience. Refer to the Needs Chart (page 233).

Now think of a situation that did not feel good at all. Was it a time when you didn't know the answer? Were people not responding as you expected them to? Were you unable to make the progress you were hoping to make, or did you get bad news that seemed to undermine everything you'd been working toward, or that you stood for?

Chances are, if you look at which needs were not getting met in the second situation, they probably have some similarity to the list you made in the more comfortable situation when you felt strong and good. Two sides of the same coin. Tuck the list away for future reference. It's just good to know what some of your needs are.

How well do you know yourself, and do you really know what makes you happy?

Jack Weil was Founder and CEO of Rockmount Ranch Wear. When people asked him what advice he would give young people starting a career, he would say, "Love your job. If you don't, change jobs, because nothing is worse than the drudgery of a job you don't like." For him, his work was his second romance, next to his marriage. Jack Weil died at the age of 107 on August 13, 2008. His grandson, Steve Weil, said of him: "He kept working all the way up to the end. He was a very inspiring person, and quite frankly, he seemed like he was in his 60s when he got into his 90s."

Marshall Goldsmith, leadership coach to top CEO's internationally, asks the question, "Who are you, and how do you know?"

You can probably recite for me whether you had a happy or difficult childhood, where you went to school or the opportunities you missed, what kind of work you do, something about your family, what your hobbies are. This tells me something about you, but it's not the deeper story. You might look at Marshall's book *MOJO: How to Get It, How to Keep It, and How to Get it Back When You Need It!* (Hyperion) to explore this topic further.

Your Most Valuable Resource

If you are like most ambitious people who start their own business, you are driven and resourceful and you will keep going until you get the job done. You probably focus more on the task at hand than on the person doing the task at hand. You just want this task to be complete so you can put on another hat and take care of the next task.

I want you to look around your office and think about the machines your business depends on. Would your business run if you didn't have a computer or a telephone? What happens when something goes wrong with them? Everything stops until you get them fixed so you can get back in business!

Now, think about the 'machine' that runs those machines ... your body! How well would the computer and telephone work if you were not there to use them, to make decisions about how to use them, to prioritize the work and get new clients and – and – and ... ?

As leader of your business, especially as a sole proprietor, your good health becomes vital. When you don't work, your clients don't receive what you've promised them, and you don't get paid.

How can you take better care of your most precious resource and still keep up with the schedule required to keep it all going? How do you take good care of your health?

You've heard it before ... exercise, get plenty of rest, drink water, take food supplements, avoid junk food, be happy. Just do it!

Maybe you're like me and you think you're cheating nature because you can stay up all night and drive yourself better than the people around you - maybe you can, and maybe it won't catch up with you. Personally, I found there was a limit to how hard I could push myself without replenishing my resources. I still keep pushing for more achievement, but I've included in my list of tasks items that keep my body healthy and strong, and activities that feed my spirit.

Back to you and what you enjoy. Here are some questions that I've found help my clients create the kind of business they will enjoy over time:

- Do you prefer to work **on your own** or **with a team**?

- Do you like to **follow a set structure** and follow the rules, or do you prefer to **create your own style** and your own rules?

- Do you appreciate **close supervision** or are you more **self directed**?

- Do you like to **set goals ahead** or just **follow your intuition**?

- Are you more comfortable having just **one product** or a **variety of options**?

- Do you **love to sell** or **hate to sell**?

- Do you prefer to **hit the ground running** or **ease into it**?

- Are you more comfortable calling on **people you already know** or a **cold market**?

- Are you more in your element in a **residential** market or a **commercial** market?

- Do you like to **follow a proven system** or **customize a system** to match you personally?

There are no right answers; only what fits you today. It may change tomorrow. It's just important to know yourself, and to be honest with yourself about what you sincerely enjoy.

Backup

You're probably the only one qualified to handle the myriad array of tasks you juggle each day to keep your enterprise going. You probably can't stop long enough to think about what would happen if you didn't show up one day. Take a moment anyway and think about this. Create backup plans. What are some strategies to keep things going if you have to step away for awhile?

The Role of Happiness

Cathy Greenberg, author *What Happy Companies Know*, asserts that being optimistic is important for leaders. She goes so far as to say that happiness equals profit. "When we looked at the 90 companies in *What Happy Companies Know*, if you take a 10% investment in capital, you will get a 3.9% ROI. If you take the same investment and invest in the people, you get greater than 8.9% return, so happiness is very profitable."

Cathy also quotes Richard Carmona, seventeenth Surgeon General of the United States, "The concepts link to executive health, organizational wellness, and the impact of rising health care costs because of stress in the workplace. Better understanding of such concepts may lead to a healthier, high-performance work-place, and possibly a happier overall work environment for human flourishing."

Cathy goes on to say, "Negative emotions such as misplaced fear are extremely debilitating, causing responses such as a feeling of victimization, entitlement, blame, and a need for rescue. It also leads to a short sighted decision making cycle: looking at just the next quarter instead of the next year. Positive emotions can re-set the brain biologically and change the culture of group dynamics. When health care costs go up, profit goes down. There is a correlation between employee satisfaction and the quality of their work. When you create an environment where people have a sense of satisfaction, the result is lower stress rate and lower costs."

Cathy Greenberg
Executive Coaching & Development
www.h2cleadership.com

It's All About You

You make your own choices, even if they're small. No one really can be in your shoes; you are the complete expert on you. Other people, like coaches, have some good ideas. Be a smart consumer and make your own choices about the ideas you implement.

Consider the possibility that you might know something about making good choices for yourself, and start small, building your confidence. Will you make some mistakes? I prefer to think of them as choices I make that give me more information so I can make different choices next time. How can you learn if you don't make choices? The more choices you make, the more times you'll miss the mark, but the better you'll get at knowing where your target is and how to get there.

♫

"If I could have half the things I've talked myself out of, I'd be a very happy man."

Colin Gautrey
Author, Coach and Facilitator
Specialising in the practical use of power and
influence in the workplace.
Political Dilemmas at Work
www.PoliticsAtWork.com

CHAPTER 7:

Customers

℘

Quick Summary:

• You can choose your customers.

• You can change your customers.

• Find customers you really enjoy being with. This will make it a pleasant experience to serve them, because you'll want to help them anyway.

Exercise:

1) Think about who you enjoy spending time with. Write down any specifics that come to mind.

2) Are there particular activities you enjoy doing with these people, and others that you don't like doing with them? Think about this and take notes.

3) What kind of people do you naturally attract? Are they people you enjoy being with? If yes, what do you like about them? If no, what don't you like about the interaction? Can you think of a way to make this win-win? Take notes.

STEP 2: YOUR CUSTOMERS

Clarify: Who is your customer?

Spend some quality time with the people you most enjoy being around and listen to them on their terms. Learn what they need, and from that perspective start thinking about what valuable improvement in their lives you can provide.

A 'customer' is more inclusive than just the people you are hoping will buy what you are selling. Think about the people who support you – your co-workers and family. They have needs too, and will be more receptive to helping you if you are interested in making their lives better first.

Who Is Your Customer?

First of all, I say YOU are the customer. You are the one who will spend the most time with your company, so make choices that work for you as well as for everyone else.

Some of your other customers:

Stakeholders
Investors
Existing customers
Potential customers
Suppliers
Regulatory agencies
Co-workers
Competitors

Your husband or wife
Your kids

Your body, your health …
Your conscience … your happiness … your values

What Is Your Customer's Goal?

Take a moment to think about what each of your customers want. Refer to the Feelings and Needs charts (page 233) to help you guess what specific customers may want.

After you have exercised your brain for awhile, check out your assumptions. Ask your customers what they need! Have a conversation! If you've guessed wrong, they'll correct you. They may correct you with gusto, but don't necessarily misinterpret this as meaning they're unhappy. Usually they are so thrilled that someone is finally listening to them that their excitement bubbles over with a lot of energy!

If they are unhappy or even angry and you're feeling safe enough, listen to them with sincere interest and compassion. If you can hear them out without being defensive, it could be a wonderful gift for both of you. You will probably gain some unexpected and valuable insight that will help propel your success with them and other customers. A truly honest conversation may even help you become clearer on your own personal goals. You may also possibly make a new friend.

Remember everyone is an individual and will respond best to you when you approach them accordingly. Read "Paul Hersey" in Section Four (page 158) for more information on Situational Leadership.

♬

"You cannot help people who do not want to be helped."

Marshall Goldsmith
Best-selling Author
What Got You Here Won't Get You There, Succession: Are You Ready? and *MOJO: How to Get It, How to Keep It, and How to Get it Back When You Need It!*
www.MarshallGoldsmithLibrary.com

CHAPTER 8:

Business

ℰ

Quick Summary:

• Choose a business you enjoy, providing a needed and valued product or service to people you enjoy being with.

• Give yourself a role you can enjoy over time.

• Remember: Just because you have a product or skill does not mean the people you want to work with will buy it.

• Also: Just because you have discovered an important need and you're ready to fill it, does not mean your target market will buy it, even if they acknowledge the need.

Exercise:

1) Spend time with people you enjoy, doing activities you enjoy. While you're doing this, listen for clues about services or products they value and don't have, or needs that aren't being fulfilled. Take notes.

2) Look at your list and take some time to consider what your favorite people need and want that you could provide.

3) Put together some ideas and talk with some of your prospects about them. Get their involvement and buy-in. If they think it's a bad idea, ask other people. If they think it's a great idea, ask if they know anyone else who might be interested.

4) Test by having an entry-level offering to sell that doesn't cost you very much to provide, and gives your customer an experience of your product or service. Then you can see how committed they are to actually buying the solution they said was so valuable to them.

STEP 3: YOUR BUSINESS

Seek out and listen to feedback about you and your business.

You may have the greatest product ever, but if the timing is not right nobody will buy. In this case you must either sign up to create a new market niche, or consider adjusting your goals to fit your customers. This does not mean there is anything wrong with your pet project. It's just about being realistic with current trends.

Regardless of who you are and what you bring to the marketplace, I suggest you actively seek input from others. You could save yourself significant time and money over the long term. Once you are better acquainted with what makes you happy and what your customers need, consider adapting your business model to match your market.

Keep your original ideas on file. I find my first ideas are often inspired and it's helpful to remember what they were when the right time finally does come around.

Don't expect yourself to be good at everything. Find strategies or other people to help you with the necessary tasks you don't do as well. If the task isn't necessary, take it off your list.

Your Business Identity
Do you know what business you are in?
Do you know why?

Have you thought about how well the design of your business matches how you like to spend your day, and the way you like to work?

Most of the time the work I do feels like fun to me. I work out of my home office, and I'm responsible to my clients for the specific projects I've agreed to do for them. It's usually something I'd like to do anyway, and I enjoy the people I surround myself with. I know it's work and I know I'm in business for myself, but I often don't notice because I just wake up in the morning and start doing things I enjoy doing.

In 1987 I opened a business in a retail setting. I had a storefront with office hours. People came to my office in the morning and expected me to be there when my sign said my office opened. If there was no work to do, I stayed in the office anyway because if a customer came through the door, they needed to find me behind my desk waiting for them. If a customer came in at the end of the day and needed something first thing the next morning, I'd probably stay late and complete the work, even if I'd spent most of the day waiting for customers that didn't show up ... actually, *especially* if there were no other customers that day, because I needed the revenue!

That experience helped me learn some things about myself. First of all, I was very bored waiting in my office. I realized I liked more flexibility than a retail storefront would allow. Second, it was more difficult to choose my customers based on who I enjoyed spending time with, and the work I enjoyed doing. It was a good learning experience, I made adjustments and now I'm happier in my business.

However, the retail storefront was a step closer to my heart than the job I've held just previously at a large corporation in Minnesota. I left Minnesota one winter in January. I was so done with winter that I left in a blizzard and just kept driving south until I got to Texas. Gradually I made my way to southern California, where I set up the retail storefront in a small beach town. I could see the ocean from my desk. The beach was about two blocks away, so I'd walk there during lunch.

One day during lunch at my Minnesota corporate job I told a co-worker that I was thinking of moving to California. She immediately said, "You can't do that!" It wasn't that she would miss me; it was that our culture said our place was there in the snow to suffer like everyone else, and who was I to think I was better than they were? I don't think I'm better than anyone else, but I did bring my nameplate from my corporate desk job and put it on my desk across the street from the beach. It turns out I *could* do that!

Something Different

Maggie Mistal gave me the following for you from her experience:

> "If you've been wanting to do something different in your career and are not sure how to go about it, try this:
>
> 1) Make a list of careers you would love to do or find triguing.
>
> 2) Write down all the questions you would like answered (for a sampling check out the online informational interviews at TheCareerProject.org).
>
> 3) Ask your network for anyone they know doing the career(s) you want. If you don't get any leads from this step, try going online to industry associations or check with your alumni association. Email or call the Executive Director and ask for any contacts he/she can recommend.

One more important point, don't make the conversation all about you. Focus instead on why your interviewee is the perfect person for you to speak with because he or she is accomplished in this field and came highly recommended. Be genuinely interested in the career path of the person you are interviewing and you will not only get information but build rapport."

Maggie Mistal
Career Consultant
www.MaggieMistal.com

Expertise

What does it take to be an expert in your field? Recent studies have found it takes about ten years of deliberate practice to develop expertise in any particular area.

What is deliberate practice?

Geoff Colvin, author of *Talent is Overrated* lists elements of deliberate practice routines which have led to world-class expertise:

- Designed by an expert specifically to improve performance
- Can be repeated often
- Feedback on results is continuously available
- Highly demanding mentally
- Is not much fun, because we constantly practice what we need to improve

Characteristics:

- **Perceiving more** (understanding the significance of indicators that average performers don't even notice, looking further ahead, knowing more from less input,

making finer distinctions than average performers)
- **Knowing more**
- **Remembering more**

Application:

- Know where you want to go
- Practice directly in the work
- Deepen your knowledge

Geoff Colvin
Author of *Talent is Overrated*

For more information:

Outliers by Malcolm Gladwell
Little, Brown
ISBN 978-0-316-01792-3

Talent is Overrated by Geoff Colvin
Penguin Porfolio
ISBN 978-1-59184-224-8

Focus

&

Quick Summary:

• Keeping the administrative side of your business running smoothly is very important.

• If this isn't your forte, find someone who is good at this to help you.

• If this is your forte, monitor yourself so you don't spend all of your time tracking no activity – be sure the sales function and other needs of your business get as much of your attention as the details.

• Be sure you keep track of promises you make, and schedule a time you'll follow through as promised.

Exercise:

1) Make a list of everything you keep track of in a spreadsheet program.

2) Add a column to the left, and label it "category". Add a category to each line.

3) Add a new column to the left, and label it "activity". For each item, type 'email', 'phone', 'visit', 'research', etc.

4) Add another column immediately to the left of the large item description column. Label this one 'priority', and assign a priority

to each line item. You can use A, B, C, and A1, B3, even Z for those you decide don't need to be on the list right now, or if they are already completed and you want to keep them on the list.

5) You can now sort this list by priority, activity, and category. Add other columns as needed.

6) Make a backup copy, and use it as a working document, making changes as you think of new items, as priorities change, and as you check things off.

STEP 4: FOCUS IS VITAL

Focus on tasks that are most important.

How well do you keep track of your time and resources? Do you know how you spend each hour? Or do you begin each day running and reacting and just keep going until there is no day left and you are exhausted?

Are you spending most of your time on your most important tasks? Create a list every night of the next day's most important tasks or priorities. Include both personal and business goals. If the list is too long, make it shorter or circle the one or two items that will make the most difference. Think about what is urgent, and what is important. Give more time to what's important.

Then schedule 20 minutes to one hour of quiet, uninterrupted time at the beginning of the day to focus on just those few items. Do not multi-task during this hour. Just make progress on your most important items.

Do this every day, the same time each day. Let people know which part of your day you are available, and which part of the day your door is closed and your phone unanswered. You can create a system in case there is an emergency during that hour, but usually the world can adjust and allow an hour for concentrated, focused work.

What's involved in running a business, and how do you keep track of all the details?

Which elements can you delegate to someone else, and which functions are best carried out by you personally?

How do you decide how to allocate your precious resources?

We can start with a focusing strategy familiar to all of us.

Leveraging Intention

In January are you like most people, thinking about your New Year's resolutions? And are you like most people ... by December has even the memory of what your January resolutions were faded?

I make no judgments here. Anytime you take a moment to look at your life and consider what to do in the future, it's a major win.

It's too easy to keep moving through life, doing the same thing day after day, using well-worn strategies to avoid the pain of familiar things not working, and letting the years pass as we all grow older. Life is hard enough without stirring things up and making changes. Or so it seems.

We do grow older. Kids learn from what we do more than what we say, so if we're meeting our problems with angry outbursts, drugs or alcohol, or distancing ourselves from the world, so will they. If we have given up on our dreams, they will not know how to find their own. If we settle for an uninspired life within the confines of what our early conditioning allowed us to explore, the world will never benefit from our true inner gifts, and we will always know we missed the part of life that could have been the most satisfying.

But it's hard to shake things up. Our schedules are already overflowing. We are already behind in so many important projects. Why add one more thing to the list?

First of all, there are ways to create new habits that don't take a lot of time, and that can have tremendous payoffs.

Second, it's worth it to trade in a well-honed habit that takes you somewhere unsatisfying for a new habit that takes you somewhere more fun.

So if I have the intention of making some improvement in my life, how do I get from January's resolutions to December's results? Incorporate Marshall's advice into your thinking:

"What am I willing to change now? Not in a few months. Not when I get caught up. Now. Then get started on the activity within two weeks, or take it off the list. And quit tormenting yourself!"

Marshall Goldsmith, Best-selling author
What Got You Here Won't Get You There
www.MarshallGoldsmithLibrary.com

Leverage those intentions by creating some simple accountability that will help you stay focused on your goal. The purpose … to help you remember to make a different choice when your old habit is ready to pull you into old results, and to give you a measurement in December so you can see your new results! Read about Peer Coaching and Daily Questions (page 153).

♬

"As a business owner, you are the single most important factor in your business. You are the only asset you have in the beginning. You are the bank account, sales staff, worker bee—you are it.'

'If you use yourself up, there is nothing left to run your business. It's essential you learn how to balance yourself, put support systems in place, and learn to get enough energy in your day to get through it.'

'Most sole proprietors just throw themselves into the work and neglect themselves. They don't realize they have to take care of themselves first. It's like the oxygen masks on the airlines ... you have to put yours on first, because you have to survive for the business to survive.'

'This would include learning what your strengths are and accepting them. Don't fight it. Your strengths are what will make your business great. Think about who you can have come alongside you to fill in your gaps.'

'I've seen people waiting for what I call 'assistant nirvana'. They think they either have to afford a full time assistant or do it themselves. I'm a fan of 'don't spend money you don't have', but there are so many other options than spending your important time on details. You kind of have to cobble it together for awhile ... an intern two hours/day after school who can file, organize client lists on your computer ... a stay at home mom who makes calls for you ... a professional organizer two hours/month ... a way to move something forward that will give you a little more stability, a little more structure, so you can win at something else.

Cynthia Jurado
Business Coach
www.arcleadershipdynamics.com

♫

"The two essentials on everyone's to-do list are exercise and hobbies. We have to stop viewing these as indulgent luxuries. Exercise is one of the best tools we can use to take care of ourselves so we can operate efficiently. Physical activity relates directly to self-esteem because we feel confident when we look and feel good. Our self-worth increases and we feel more powerful when we can do more because we have more energy."

Saundra Pelletier
Speaker and author of *Saddle Up Your Own White Horse*
www.SaundraPelletier.com

See Also:

Resources to Help You Focus:

CHAPTER 10

Sales

ℰꙶ

Quick Summary:

• For any business to be successful, someone has to sell something.

• If this isn't your forte, find someone who is good at this to help you.

• If this is your forte, make sure you are keeping track of the promises you make, and find someone to help you with the details.

• If you feel shy about promoting yourself, focus instead on the message.

• Make only commitments you can keep.

• Have a professional business card.

Exercise:

1) Look at your promotional materials and messages in various mediums. Are they consistent? Are the claims accurate? Are you using benefit statements? Do they address the needs of your target audience? Do they look and sound attractive and compelling to your target audience?

2) Really listen to your customers. Find out how they heard about you. Do more of that.

3) Ask your happy customers for referrals.

STEP 5: SOMEONE HAS TO SELL

Sell your personal brand along with your product.

For any business to be successful, someone has to sell something. If you're managing your career, you are selling your personal brand. If you're shy, join Toastmasters or get involved with a professional group. Practice talking with people. Think about what you have to offer professionally, and learn to convey this in brief statements people will respond to with interest.

How likeable are you? Do people trust you? Read *What Got You Here Won't Get You There* by Marshall Goldsmith and see if you can discover ways to become more effective in your interactions.

Do you like to sell, or hate to sell?

Be honest about it, and be sure you are always doing something to promote your business. I've found it takes about two years of promotion until new business starts coming in by itself, and consistent promotion makes a big difference.

Marshall Goldsmith is one of the most successful individual entrepreneurs I know. He is one coach, and his business activities all revolve around him being a coach. Yet he has a very successful international business, and his name has become a recognizable brand worldwide. How did he do this?

Well, aside from his eight million+ frequent flier miles, his endless energy meeting with clients, speaking to thousands of people in audiences throughout the world, and having written over 20 books, he is continually promoting himself and his work. When I met him in 2002 his schedule was full and he had an 8-month waiting list for coaching clients. Someone asked him why he kept promoting his services when he was already so successful. His answer, "My calendar is full *because* I continue to promote my work."

Where do your customers come from? Referrals are the best

source. Who do your happy customers know that could use your services, and would they mind introducing you to them?

There are many ways to get the word out.

When you're in business for yourself, your business associates are the network of professionals who help you develop and maintain your business, your customers, and your potential customers ... in short, everyone.

Do you have a presentation ready that demonstrates the value potential customers will receive, describes your products and services clearly, and gives the listener a clear next step to begin working with you? What can you say in 15 seconds on an elevator, and what can you say in a one-hour sales presentation? Be prepared for either, and anything in between.

On Paper

Start by creating a flier. The following will help you think through what you want to say. Later you can adapt your printed message to other mediums. Make sure you create a professional business card you feel proud to hand people you meet.

Sheryl Roush, an experienced graphic designer and speaker, asked me to share the following with you:

Marketing Your Services in Print:
3 Stages for Designing an Effective Flyer

You are talented, have great expertise, and offer a valuable service to others. How do you get their attention and generate a response?

When creating any promotion, begin by placing yourself in your potential BUYER'S shoes, think like THEY think. Become your buyer. A big mistake in most promotional pieces is that they are designed from the SELLER'S point-of-view. What is their "pain" and how is your service the "solution?"

There are three stages of rapport required in any promotion: 1) Relevance; 2) Confirmation; and 3) Action. These stages must be done in order for your promotion to be effective.

Stage 1. In the first 1-7 seconds the buyer is looking for the relevance of your service, the benefits, or "WIIFM?" Placed in the top one-third of your layout, the reader browses short body copy, graphics, images, and color. Name their pain in the form of a question to compel them to read further. Since 70-80% of readers are "skimmers" and quick decision makers, use subheads and bullets for this group.

Stage 2 is up to 90 seconds, where your reader is still trying to decide whether this is a "match" for them, or not. Avid readers continue reading the piece and require longer body text plus all the facts and details to make a well-informed decision. Consider adding testimonials from satisfied buyers. This stage utilizes the middle portion of the layout and toward the bottom of the layout.

Stage 3 is vital in your promotion. Based on how engaged your buyer is and how well you have addressed their needs in the first two stages, the reader will naturally "flow" into this bottom one-third of the layout. This is the Call to Action stage, where you instruct the reader how to respond affirmatively to what they have read. This is the best place for your logo, email, toll free phone number, website. Create a "sense of urgency" using bold italics (i.e., Call today for your free 15-minute consultation!).

After you finish your draft, show it to others, ideally in your target market. How easily do they follow it? Is it compelling enough for them to take action? What is missing? What can be removed? Is it buyer-centered? Minimize the use of "we" and "our" and maximize "your" and "you" in the copy and headlines.

To generate higher response, use all three stages in any promotion you create!

Sheryl Roush, International Trainer on Marketing Design and Author of *Solid Gold Newsletter Design*
www.SparklePresentations.com

Online

I've been working with the Internet and online marketing since 1996. Things have changed a bit since then, and I expect they will change more by the time you're reading this book. If I explain something technical to you right now, some element of what I'm explaining will probably change by the time I've finished writing the sentence.

So I won't go into anything technical. There are some principles I've learned that stood me well in the 90s that still hold up today, and I expect these principles will continue to be useful in the future. I will keep more updated information on my website, www.CoachMarilyn.com. You can also check out my book Social Media for Small Business: Tips on Using Your Time Effectively. Here are some ways to think about your online promotion:

1) Don't put anything online that you would not want said about you in front of your boss, your co-workers, your spouse, your children. Honesty and integrity count here, too. One world flows into another, as people who search on your name or business name will find everything that is out there about you. It's a lot like a small town.

2) Be careful about playing technical tricks with the search engines. Some strategies are useful because they help search engines determine the topic of your content. Other strategies can get you black-listed. Strategies like putting thousands of keywords in colored text the same color as the page background color were out of date by 1999. Don't do that. Just try to play it straight, and use title tags, header tags, and meta tags to describe the actual content on your web page. Make the content easy to read, and filled with valuable information for the reader. Use key words throughout the content, in context. When you create a link, make sure the words you are linking go to a page with content that is congruent with the words in the link. And so on. Congruence between what you say the page is about and the actual content on the page is important. That's the magic here.

3) Don't misuse email lists to spam, and don't abuse the hospitality of networking and discussion sites to sell yourself in a way that offends the members. Get to know the members honestly, find out what they need, and offer a solution if you have one. Just like the real world. Be respectful, polite, and make real connections with like-minded people. The rest will follow.

4) Your online promotion probably will not replace your other forms of promotion, but simply enhance and augment them. Putting your website url on your printed material allows people to follow up at their convenience in a non-threatening way as

they look over what you've put on your website. If they find this reassuring, or they find what they are looking for, they may give you a call or stop by, or take the next step in the call to action on your website.

In Person

As head of your organization, you are your organization's image and reputation. What do your business associates see about your business when they interact with you? How do they feel about coming back to you and your company? This is your best and most powerful advertising. Learn how to handle some of the tough situations that can come your way.

Preparing a presentation:

• What is your purpose?

• Who is the audience?

• Outline key points in simple language.

• Practice, practice, practice.

• Copy any handouts.

• Practice in the meeting room if possible.

• Get there early.

Questions to ask yourself when preparing your presentation:

1) Credibility: What gives me the right to talk about this?

2) What can I say in the first 60 seconds to get their attention?

3) What are some stories to illustrate my points?

4) What do I want the audience to do or feel at the end of my presentation?

(Notes from **Dave Almos'** course "Innovation in Business"
San Diego 2008)

♬

"What suggestions do I have for someone starting a new business? Do your homework! Then try a couple of things, and finally put your resources into what works."

Jess Serrano
Co-Owner, Studio 69 Hair Salon
San Diego, CA

CHAPTER 11

Follow-up & Delivery

ഇ

Quick Summary:

• Be curious about how your customers perceive their experience with you and your company and products, and ask for their valuable feedback.

• Be ready to make changes to show your customers that you are sincere about your desire to improve.

• If you can't make the improvement, tell your customers why, and let them know you value their business.

Exercise:

1) Ask your customers about their experience with you. Tell them you would like to improve, and ask if they have any suggestions.

2) Remember to just listen without any judgment or hurt feelings. Keep in mind, you are sincerely interested, and the only way to find out is to ask. Take notes.

3) Thank them for their candor and willingness to share.

STEP 6: FOLLOW-UP & DELIVERY

Ask how you are doing and deliver on your promises.

Now you have your customers, you have your business and your product or service. How are you doing on the delivery side?

Are you clear about what you have promised your customers?

Are you there when they look for you?

What can you do to improve your business in your customers' eyes?

Resist the urge to just keep going along the same track without asking your customers how you're doing. Why not ask? People like being asked for their opinion. It conveys respect and appreciation, which is what you want your customers to feel when they think of you.

There is so much valuable information to be gained by asking. Whether what your customers say is accurate or inaccurate, remember that you are listening for their perception and they are the ones writing the check.

Even if they have a negative perception, you need to know what they are thinking. If you ask the question, they can let you know the problem, and you have a chance to fix it. If you can't fix it, you can at least let them know how much you value the relationship.

Feedback

How do we know who we are in the world?

We can see in the eyes of the people around us how they view us ... if we're paying attention.

Most of us don't relish the idea of 'feedback' ... we have had too much experience with what sounded like criticism, judgment, analysis. We have responded with longwinded explanations which not only went unappreciated, but seemed to actually fuel distance between us and our intended message, and our desired connection and rapport with the other person.

Read about Feed*Forward* (page 153).

You Can Fire a Customer

I used to think only employees could be fired, and I used to think a customer could choose not to do business with me, but that I didn't have the same right to choose not to work with a particular customer. I've found it's very important to both me and my customers that I'm honest about whether or not the relationship is working out.

There may be some legal considerations depending upon your industry. I will leave that up to you and your attorney. I'm just going to talk about the personal management side of things.

You may know it's time for you as the leader to step in and do something about a customer that is not working out. This is not your favorite thing. Where do you start?

I say first take your time to get real clear with yourself. What is it that you really need and want from that person or role right now? Try to go a little deeper with your own understanding of yourself, because that will help you get what you need in the process. Make a list of specific behaviors and requests so the person knows exactly what you want from them, and where things are not going so well from your perspective.

Go into this with an open heart and be willing to learn something new from this offending customer you are probably pretty frustrated with by now. Acknowledge your feelings to yourself and leave them and your judgments at the door so you can have an honest conversation with this person.

Listen with sincere interest as the other person (if they feel safe enough with you), reveals what is going on for them. If the words you hear push your buttons, take a deep breath and remember it's not about you; they are just expressing their needs in the best way their skills allow. They are just talking about themselves. If you're interested in developing the relationship, why not be interested in what is unique about this person?

Then decide together your next step. Consider being creative. You are the captain steering the boat; allow them to inform your decision because respect and trust can build long-term commitment, or perhaps an advocate if parting is the best course.

Do we really need more enemies in our lives? I prefer to create more friends.

♫

"You become the star when you listen, because listening validates the other person."

Oprah Winfrey
Media Mogul and Philanthropist
"Oprah" Television Show 2008
www.Oprah.com

CHAPTER 12

Review & Celebrate

ଚଠ

Quick Summary:

• The business world is constantly changing. Be willing to adjust your business model accordingly without undermining what is currently successful for you.

• Life and business are easier when you're having fun. Take time to celebrate, both at the end of a project, and all throughout the process.

• Thank the people who have helped you.

Exercise:

1) Stay on top of market changes in your industry.

2) Constantly ask yourself if this affects your business, or if it could in the future.

3) Make notes about possible strategies that you can refer to as needed in the future.

4) Make changes if needed.

5) Make sure you have at least some fun every day, so you stay lighthearted and inspired.

6) Think about your customers and do something to add fun, pleasure or appreciation to their day.

STEP 7: REVIEW & CELEBRATE

Review your business so far, celebrate and have some fun.

Life and business are easier when you are having fun. People are more attracted to you when you are light-hearted and inspired. Remember what makes you happy, and include it as part of your day. Think about what makes your customers happy, and spend part of your day doing something fun for them you know they will appreciate. That little extra really makes a difference.

Recalibrate: Alignment with Goals

Remember your original vision, before life got so complicated with new business, new issues, new opportunities?

How are you doing in terms of following your original plan? As a matter of fact, does your original plan still fit the marketplace, and have you learned anything new about how you really want to spend your day?

Does anything need to be updated? How will you make edits to your original plan without losing important ground?

Chris Coffey offered the following for this book. This is the review process he uses with his coaching clients:

After Action Review:
What did you set out to do?
Why?
What actually happened?
Why did it happen?
What insights did you have?
What are you going to do moving forward?

Chris Coffey
Keynote Speaker, Leadership Coach and Trainer
www.ChristopherCoffey.com

Our economic world is changing very rapidly. It's imperative to keep checking back with our own personal business assumptions regularly, and be prepared to adjust our business choices as our market and our business environment change.

Pitfalls to Avoid

I asked David G. Thomson, author of Blueprint to a Billion, what characteristics help a leader grow their business from startup to $50 million.

> "A leader would need to be a fast worker, a fast problem solver, able to build a team dynamically, and able to share leadership for their idea with their team. You have to find your other half, and give that person actual power" (see inside/outside leadership in Blueprint to a Billion).'

> 'In my research I found the odds of failure were greater than the odds of success, and I discovered three common pitfalls:

> **First Pitfall:** Beware the founder or inventor who has an idea they cannot explain in terms customers and investors can understand.

> **Second Pitfall:** Beware the founding or engineering team that believes their own hype.

> **Third Pitfall:** Get people in the boat who are really on board.'

> 'I found the people with the most passion tended to go out of business, because they never knew when

to let go of an idea that was not working. It is like walking through a maze. You do come to dead ends when you walk through a maze, and you have to be wise enough to turn around rather than continuing to hit your head against the wall.'

'In terms of leadership, you have to be flexible, and you want to be passionate, but it is important to be passionate and have goals toward the direction of the idea rather than the specific idea. You start your business with a specific model in mind. Your initial model will evolve based on what you learn along the way. You have to be flexible enough to reshape your idea as you listen to customers, so you deliver something that is highly valued.'

'As a leader, you have to be flexible, humble, and a good listener. You want to have a balance between passion and pragmatism or reality. You want to have good problem solving skills, and you want to have integrity.'

'When you do not have that foundation, you may start to grow a company, but invariably you fail. You have to be consistent about this while you go from one million to one billion. It is about being consistent over a long time frame in a consistent way with a consistent set of values."

David G. Thomson
Author, *Blueprint to a Billion*
Business Advisor to Growth Companies
www.BlueprintGrowth.com

Celebrate

You have been dreaming big and working hard.

You have stretched and found new ways to accomplish goals you were not so sure you could achieve.

It's time to take a moment to enjoy the benefits of your labor.

Is everything perfect?

Have you accomplished everything according to plan?

Are you everything you would like to be?

Probably not!

That is part of the process. Celebrate the mystery too, because you have probably gained some real treasures that were not on your list either.

Take a moment and rest. Thank everyone who has helped you.

Especially yourself.

Give yourself a day off and spend it exactly the way you want.

♫

"I believe if you do anything with passion, there is a success behind it."

Marie Osmond on The Larry King Show 2008

What I can do today to stay lighthearted and inspired:

How I can bring fun, pleasure or appreciation to my customers today:

Recession or Plenty

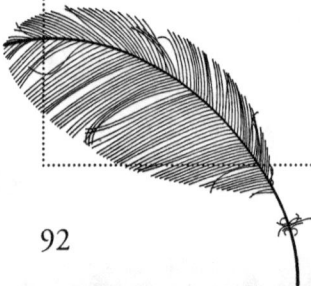

Stories

Real stories of people I have known.

Some of the names and details have been changed.

Life experience spans many categories, so it was difficult for me to insert these stories into any particular chapter.

Please enjoy the stories for what they are … an honest mix of recession and plenty.

I've made some comments at the beginning of the stories that may serve as a guide for dealing with some of the elements in the particular stories. As with everything else in this book, take what works for you and discard the rest.

CHAPTER 13:

Bill

Recovery

℘

Quick Summary:

Bill has had a successful career in the corporate world. Three years ago he was in an accident, and his work since then has been learning to walk and think again. His overwhelming needs for control and predictability in his environment have created so much stress for both him and his family that he is now living by himself in an apartment near the clinic where he continues to receive therapy. He is grateful he is now able to take care of himself, and also frustrated because he remembers what it was like to be a very successful executive. He has to keep reminding himself to be grateful for what is, and be willing to redefine himself. Now he is able to walk but has difficulty standing for very long, and he is able to think but needs information in small doses in a step by step process. When he gets overwhelmed, he needs to withdraw and regroup.

Bill is **in the business of:** creating a life post-injury.

Exercise:

If this is you:

• Life brings us many opportunities, some more challenging than others. As life happens, just remember this is part of the process and make peace with what is.

• Take stock honestly of what resources you will need to recover from the setback, and give yourself those resources. Be creative as needed.

• Allow yourself to consider the possibility any changes you need to make to your accustomed lifestyle or even your perception of yourself could have profound value, and assume there is a gift in there somewhere.

• Be open to letting others help you.

• Set your boundaries, and protect your environment internally and externally so you only have positive, supportive people and images of you in your wonderful future around you.

• Remember, this difficult experience is only temporary. It may take time, but eventually you will get back to some semblance of a normal life and have normal problems again like everyone else!

• Forgive the people who want to help but don't know how. Thank them for trying, and protect yourself as best you can from any extra burdens their 'help' creates for you.

If this is someone you know:

• Don't automatically label what they are going through as 'bad'. Try to just be a supportive friend without inflicting your judgments and diagnoses into the mix.

• Don't automatically assume you know what is best for them, or try to fix them or make their decisions for them, unless you know them very well and they have explicitly asked you to do this for them. If this is the case, try to give them back their autonomy and self-determination as soon as possible.

• Do listen to them on their terms, and try to understand their environment and needs from their point of view. If they tell you they need something you don't understand, take time to try and understand. Repeat back to them what you heard them say and keep guessing until they say you got it right, and then trust they do have some valid ideas about their own needs.

• When you have a sense of what they need, try to think of positive imagery, and exercises they are capable of doing in their present state, that will help them rebuild their life and capabilities again. Ask them what they are ready for, and what they would consider positive encouragement at this point in their recovery.

• Don't simply walk on eggshells around them, though you may need to adjust some of your accustomed behavior around them while they are fragile or vulnerable.

• Tell them the truth about what you are feeling and needing (page 233); don't try to mask your resentment or frustration about how hard you are working to help them, or what you are giving up … take care of your own needs, too, and tell them the truth when you need something. The message will come across even if you don't say it.

• Is there any way they can help you while you are helping them? Sometimes the smallest contribution, if it's meaningful to you and accepted and appreciated by you, can be the most wonderful medicine. It can give them evidence they are still 'valid', as opposed to being (an) 'invalid'.

∞

Bill is very grateful to be alive, and constantly reminds himself of what is going well in his life so he does not sink into discouragement and despair. He knows if he allows even one negative thought, it takes him closer to descent and death, so he is very motivated to focus on what works. He has to tell himself the truth, but sometimes he consciously decides to be in denial about how bad things are, because he knows if he allows himself to fully take in the whole story, that will only diminish his ability to use his limited personal resources to continue his upward recovery.

He misses his family, and is always glad when they visit … when he is expecting it in advance. He finds he can accomplish quite a lot of thinking when he can trust his environment will remain quiet and uninterrupted.

He has long since given up on anger, though sometimes the disappointment of not being able to do something he wants to do is so great the anger comes anyway. When it does, he reminds himself that being angry will only use up precious energy he would rather allocate to something he actually can do in his current condition. He tries not to judge anything. This has been an education in accepting the conditions of the moment, and finding something he can do in each moment to feel productive, or like he is moving forward, or feeling happy. At times when all he can do is go back to bed and be quiet in a dark room, he reminds himself he is getting stronger, and that teaching himself to recover from whatever challenge just kicked his butt will help him recover faster the next time.

Bill's self-concept is still quite fragile, though he never cared much about what other people thought of him before he got hurt. He wants to try new things and meet new people, especially when he hears of opportunities that he knows he would love to be a part of. He does not discount the possibility of being able to do this someday, and is willing for now to focus on smaller opportunities. He avoids people who are critical or who see the negative side of things. He chooses to be with people who are upbeat and see the possibilities.

In his more sensitive state, he has learned something about communication that he expects to benefit from when he is 'back in the normal world'. He has discovered that unexpressed strong feelings convey a more powerful message than words, and usually sound threatening. He gathers people around him who can deliver a simple, direct, honest message. If they are frustrated because he forgot and asked them for the same thing they had just done for him, they don't swallow their frustration and 'act nice'. They respectfully tell him the truth. "I'm not sure I want to do that for you again. I just did it for you yesterday. Are you sure you need it?"

It's easier for him to understand a clear message congruent with feelings, even though it's negative, than a barrage of unexpressed strong feelings, regardless of the words being said. It all needs to be interpreted, and it's like getting ten messages at once and the feelings come through first. That is adding an extra burden to an already compromised 'receiver system'!

He does have his basic living needs taken care of. He gets help with the shopping, and he makes food that does not require much of his attention. He can get around the apartment and keep things clean. He has a desk with easy access to his favorite office equipment, some of which he still can't use, but he knows someday he will find it useful.

His next goal is to start working again. He knows he isn't ready to take a regular job with a company, but he had some experience in college running a business. He's willing to start small and give it a try.

What can he do to make this work, and what does he need help with?

Most important, what does he enjoy doing, that he is able to do now, that someone will buy? And how much can he promise to produce without stressing himself out and going backward in his recovery?

Luckily through his recovery he is beginning to realize that productivity does not define him, and he no longer connects his self worth and self image with his work. For now he is just looking for something he will enjoy and be capable of producing over time. At least for now.

So what can he do? He can walk and think when it's quiet and he is not in tremendous pain. He is having difficulty learning new things cognitively. He does not need to earn money to survive (yet), but he will feel better moving more into the flow of the life he used to know, and being a more productive part of society.

He has a computer that he can use part of every day if he gets some new furniture that gives him the ability to sit in different positions and work different areas of his body throughout the day.

He enjoys painting. Maybe he could buy some watercolors, paper and a table easel. That actually sounds like more fun right now.

He loves dogs, but is not strong enough to be a dog-walker or even dog-sit for the neighbors. Maybe that will come in time.

He follows the stocks every day and knows the market well, but realizes he is emotionally susceptible to the market ups and downs, and he doesn't want to add that extra burden to his environment just now.

He thinks about what activities would actually be therapeutic for him. He decides to try becoming a watercolor artist. This would help him express the pent-up feelings he knows he hasn't dealt with from the many changes in his life the past few years, and it doesn't cost much for supplies or take up much room in his apartment.

How can he make money? He does have a friend with an art gallery in another city, and there are several art galleries close by. Maybe the clinic would show his art. As he thinks about this he realizes he would truly value some response from the world that he has something valuable to offer. It has been so long! Even if no one buys anything, to see his art on the walls anywhere would give him a lift.

He decides to take it one more step, to make the effort to learn something new. He hit his head in the accident, and his thinking has been somewhat scrambled and vague ever since, though it has been improving of late. He knows it will be challenging, and he may or may not be able to do it, but he decides to learn how to build a website to sell his artwork. One step at a time. No pressure. It won't hurt to try to learn something new, and even the attempts will be therapeutic.

Bill sits down at his desk and begins to make a list of the supplies he'll need, and a step by step list of what to do, while his house is still quiet. He writes down names of support people next to certain tasks, "Mark – buy art supplies" "Judy – buy a timer for me so I will remember when to eat and take my medicine" and "Judy – help me create a schedule of when I work and when I get therapy, and anything else I need to keep my life going" "George – look over my plans to see if I've missed anything important".

It's wonderful to have friends!

It's wonderful to be alive!

CHAPTER 14

Richard and Sharon
Exploring New Roles
ℰℷ

Quick Summary:

Richard is in a role at work that he finally gives up on. He makes a plan to start his own business and does it the right way: starting small on the side and gradually building his side income so it covers his expenses, building cushions so he is okay when he leaves his job. He finds he is not so sure he wants to leave his job after all in the end, because by looking at himself and what he loves and going after it, he got some of his needs met and finds he actually enjoys his job.

Sharon has been making dinner each night for her family because she 'has to'. She hates cooking, and one day as she listens over dinner to the members of her family talking about their wonderful days after she spent her day doing domestic chores, she reaches the end of her patience. She blows up, decides she is no longer making dinner, and she spends the evening writing up a chart of domestic chores with a schedule so everyone contributes. She gets up the next morning and realizes, even though she has freed herself from her domestic burdens, she now needs to deal with her underlying habit of blaming and feeling resentful. She learns to think in terms of what she wants, instead of what she does not want.

Richard is **in the business of:** creating a business of his own. Sharon is **in the business of:** creating a foundation for life that can sustain and guide her to a more satisfying role in her life.

Exercise:

If this is you:

• Go through the 7 Steps (page 30) in order to take inventory and create a plan that supports what matters to you individually.

• Take time to communicate with each other as you go through the process.
• Ask how you can support each other's needs and dreams.

• Ask how you can be a better husband or wife.

• Make time to have fun, and celebrate the little things together.

If this is someone you know:

• Refrain from trying to give advice.

• See if you can listen and be supportive of their process individually and as a team.

• Simply keep encouraging them that they will find their answers.

❦

The day Richard realized he'd had enough was in another one of the endless meetings at work when nothing seems to happen and he knows his boss is going to want his report by the end of the day, but because of the meetings his boss insists he attends, Richard has no time to do research for the report. Should he just throw some numbers together and get the report in on time, or challenge his boss on the larger issue and ask for research time so he can have good numbers for his report?

Either way Richard is just tired of the constant need to manage everyone else's responsibilities and personalities. He just wants to do his job, and he wishes his manager would create an environment that protects him from all of these distractions so he can focus on the reports listed in his job description.

Not usually prone to daydreaming, his attention starts to wander and he finds himself thinking about model trains. The first time he saw a model train as a kid he couldn't believe it. He watched the train go around the track for hours, with the bigger kids adding tracks and changing switches, and the train either finding its way through the new maze, or falling off the track so the kids had to put it back on and try again. One time the train derailed right in front of him, so he actually touched the cars and helped put them back on the track, too. It was thrilling.

Hmm … maybe he could start his own business … maybe it could have something to do with trains! That thought led to another, and on his way home that night he started making a list of all the things he could research to see if his idea would work. He got on the computer that night and decided there was enough evidence to take the next step. He found a local group of enthusiasts who were meeting the following week, so he showed up and began networking.

He listened to the members and came up with a plan for his new product. He asked for their feedback, and made some adjustments based on what he learned. Some of them had connections in other parts of the country, so he took down names and contacted everyone that week. One of the new contacts was in charge of the industry newsletter, so Richard purchased an ad in an edition six months in the future, giving himself enough time to develop his offering.

Though this new venture was compelling, he looked at his family budget and decided he would have to start his business part time, during evenings and weekends. He would have less TV time, but he could keep his exercise program going. He knew his wife would complain if he didn't schedule some time with her, so he scheduled Tuesday evenings free because he knew there would not be any conflicts with local model train happenings.

"I'm going into a new business!" he announced at dinner the next night. His wife, Sharon, looked at him blankly. He told her about his research and his plans with great enthusiasm. "I'll do this on the side, so this means I'll still be going to my job during the day, and I can do this on the weekend and evenings during the week." Still no response from Sharon, so he went on proudly, "And I even scheduled time for us. I'm keeping every Tuesday evening open so we can have some time together, just you and me."

Sharon sat silent for awhile, absentmindedly picking up the pieces of corn and carrots their son, Billy, had just dropped on the floor. Then she put her napkin on the table, stood up, walked to the kitchen, leaned against the counter, and just stood there. She looked around her at the stove with the remnants of dinner she had prepared, the pile of dishes in the sink that was clean and empty moments before her children and husband arrived home. She looked beyond the kitchen to the living room scattered with their belongings that, again, had been clean before they arrived.

Sharon wanted to say something positive to encourage her husband. She heard his excitement and knew how much he loved model trains, and she wanted him to be happy. But something inside her had shifted, and she was not sure herself what was going on. She knew suddenly that she was not happy.

"I guess that's a good thing," she finally managed to say. "Yes, good, if that makes you happy." She was ready to say, "Whatever I can do to help," but she couldn't get the words out. Instead she washed her hands, left the dishes in the sink and the pots on the stove and her unfinished supper on the table, and walked outside to the back porch. She looked at her favorite chair that she rarely used, and sat down. She just sat and looked and stared into space for awhile. Then suddenly it came to her.

Everyone else in her family had talked about their wonderful day, and what they had learned and how they had explored new territory. She had cleaned the house, washed their clothes, and taken care of their errands. She had nothing to say about what she had learned today, or how she had been inspired. She suddenly noticed how empty she felt, and with a big sigh, she sat back and closed her eyes. What could she do to change this situation?

She had always wanted to take an art class. Whatever else she had enjoyed doing earlier in her life, she had long forgotten about. But she could take an art class. That was a start.

Another thing she could do is get help with the household chores. Everyone could pitch in. She stood right up and found Billy's markers and a large piece of paper, and she made a chart with everyone's name on it. Down the left side she made a list of all the chores she had done that day, and she made assignments for everyone. By her name she wrote "vacation". She put the chart up on the refrigerator door, gave her husband and children a kiss on the cheek, went back to her chair on the porch and fell asleep. Richard gently woke her later and they put the children to bed and fell asleep in each other's arms.

The next morning, when the alarm clock went off and Richard got up, she turned over and went back to sleep. She woke up two hours later, and the house was silent. She was alone. There was nothing on her 'to do' list today. She paused, thinking. She decided to take a long bath. Next she made herself a beautiful breakfast and sat at the patio table, watching the birds play by the pool. Her mind went from the pool to the many times Richard had promised to take the family to the beach, and a long litany of other broken promises. She started feeling resentful, and the feeling began to cast a shadow on her otherwise perfect day. Finally she called her long-time friend Ann and told her all the news.

Ann chuckled at Sharon's antics, and grew silent when she heard Sharon's litany of blame. "Sharon," she said seriously. "You sound like you did before you got married! Everything was someone else's fault. Pull yourself together! It's a great day! How about we have lunch together?"

During lunch Ann brought Sharon back to reality, and helped Sharon remember techniques she had used earlier in her life to stop blaming, and to take responsibility for herself. Sharon sighed with relief. Luckily she had caught herself before Richard got home and she unfairly unloaded all of this on him. Apparently so many years of neglecting her own needs had brought old habits of thought back to be addressed. Once through that phase, Ann and Sharon started brainstorming about what Sharon could do with her new life. Art classes were a great start. A trip to the local community college yielded a course catalog of art classes with oils and watercolors, and computers. Sharon had missed the computer era while everyone else in her family used them with ease, so Sharon decided to sign up for a computer class for graphic designers.

Meanwhile, Richard juggled his usual morning routine with the children's needs. He managed to follow the checklist Sharon had put on the refrigerator, and everyone somehow got out of the house on time. He was not as frustrated during the day as he attended his usual schedule of meetings. He found himself in casual conversation with his manager about needing time to do proper research for the reports, instead of the formal, confrontational meeting Richard had been contemplating for months. His manager looked surprised and quickly removed Richard from three projects that held the most meetings. He gave Richard an extra report to manage.

Richard left work that day with a new sense of freedom. His work situation was going better, plus he had his model train project in the works. As months went by, his day job remained steady as he was able to focus mainly on reports, and he had adequate time to do background research. On the other hand, his model train business was getting out of hand. So many different kinds of things to take care of. Supplies didn't show up when they were supposed to. Three of his contacts had three different ideas of how something should be done, and he had ended up in the middle of it. Now it was time to send in his ad copy to the newsletter, and he wasn't ready. He knew what he wanted to say, but he had no idea how to say it.

As Richard juggled his job and new venture, Sharon was having fun taking computer classes. She learned how to create digital art, and how to create ads in a business class she took for fun. Watching Richard struggle with pen and paper one night after dinner, she asked if she could help. He looked at her hopefully and they went to work together. Within an hour they had an ad they were both proud of.

Richard hesitated before asking her the next question. He knew Sharon had wonderful people skills, and he had thought of her wistfully several times as he had tried to make sense of what his model train colleagues wanted. Would she come with him to the next meeting?

She looked up, surprised and pleased. Yes, of course she would!

They put their children to bed, and went to sleep in each other's arms again.

CHAPTER 15:

James Singletary
Second Career

$\wp$

Quick Summary:

James was finally experiencing the success he had always dreamed of, when the life and career he had worked so hard for suddenly changed direction when he got physically hurt.

He could have become bitter and wasted the rest of his life thinking about the past, and 'if only', and what he used to be.

Instead, he took his considerable character and skill and fashioned a new life and career for himself, significantly helping other people in the process.

James is **in the business of** creating a second career.

Exercise:

If this is you:

• Give yourself some time to adjust mentally and keep an open mind about your next career move.

• Go through the 7 Steps (page 45) in order to take inventory and to create a plan to support what matters to you.

• Consider the possibility there may be another career path you will enjoy as much or more than your current position.

• Think about what you would enjoy giving to others.

If this is someone you know:

• Be patient with this person. Career is often tied very closely to a person's self-concept, and the ability to earn a living is tied very closely to a basic sense of security. Give them some time and let them find their way.

• Provide consistent, unconditional support to the extent that you can, while taking care of your own needs at the same time. Yes, they have needs, and so do you. Be honest about asking for the help you need from them.

• Be understanding if they're not ready to jump back into life fully for awhile.

• They may need some structure to help them feel more secure as their world changes. Do what you can to create a predictable, positive routine ... to benefit yourself and your friend.

೮೧

James Singletary was an All-American in high school football. "As kids we all dreamt of being a football star," he remembers. "We saw that as one of our only options." When he was drafted in the NFL as a linebacker, he began a promising sports career that was soon cut short by injuries.

"It didn't really turn out like I'd hoped, but everything happens for a reason," he says.

After a couple of years soul-searching, he ran into an optometrist. After some long conversations, James decided to look more closely into becoming an optometrist himself.

"It took off from there," he says. "I'm not going to say it

was by accident, but it was probably serendipity in a way."

Singletary and his wife, Dr. Eva Shiau, now own Eye Medics. "The business is growing quickly," he says. James is building a reputation as one North Carolina's foremost specialists in Vision Training, Pediatric Vision Care and Orthokeratology.

"You can go out into the world and search for Nirvana, trying to find the perfect place, but it all starts from within, not from your surroundings. What I look for is quality of living," he says. "I try to look for things that matter, things that add substance to life, and not just chase the dollar bill."

Singletary is especially interested in eye care for young people.

"Most people don't know that your first eye exam should be at six months old," he says. "You hear about your teeth, but you seldom hear about your eyes. It's partly our fault because we haven't done a good job getting the word out. I am trying to change that, especially in my state."

"I am trying to be one of the first doctors in my area to speak to educators in schools on the importance of early comprehensive eye exams. We are actually trying to get a mobile unit together and go out to day-care centers and schools to screen kids correctly. It's been shown that screenings by pediatricians and schools are not effective in picking up visual problems."

"I'm a product of my environment," he says. "I had vision problems when I was a kid. And because of that, I was a poor student. The only way I got into college was on a football scholarship. Then, in college, they found out I had a vision problem. Once it was corrected, I started to read with comfort and then my whole life changed."

Changing a young person's life by discovering a vision problem and addressing it can have profound effects in many aspects of their performance and their ability to follow through on what interests them in life.

"That is what makes you feel good," he says. "You are actually doing something good and making a positive contribution to society. That is what it's all about."

James continues to practice optometry with his partner and wife, Dr. Eva Shiau, in Eye Medics in Fayetteville, North Carolina.

Dr. James H Singletary

Adult & Pediatric Eye Care, Behavioral/Neuro-Optometry, Vision Therapy Center
www.eyemedicsonline.com

CHAPTER 16

John and Pat Hendrickson
Team Effort

ॐ

Quick Summary:

John and Pat live with their five children in a home they recently purchased from Orange Savings and Loan. OS&L had foreclosed on the entire tract because the builder could not make the payments. John and Pat find ways to be very efficient with their resources, enlist the help of their children, and find other motivated people to join their Amway business.

Pat is **in the business of**: keeping the household together. ohn is **in the business of:** keeping the finances together. Together they are **in the business of:** creating financial stability in the near term, and financial security in the longer term.

Exercise:

If this is you:

• Take stock honestly of your resources and needs.

• Stop doing things you can no longer afford in terms of time, money, worry and blame.

• Use your energy to imagine what you want, and take steps to get there.

• Take a second look around to find resources you may not have seen before (see "Are You Leaving Valuables on the Table" page 6).

• See if you can turn any out-goes into creative resources.

• Make adjustments you can live with. Be frugal, but find ways to nurture each person's spirit.

• Use this as an opportunity to win as a team.

If this is someone you know:

• Think about community or extended family resources that might help the family, and offer to help bring those resources to the family in meaningful ways. Sometimes they are shy about asking, or just too busy to organize one more thing, even if it would be of great assistance.

• Don't think that talking about the problem and how bad things are will be of assistance. Help them focus on what is possible, and look for unexpected opportunities that make things better.

ℰↃ

After running a very successful real estate office in the Midwest, John had decided to move his family to a new market in southern California. It is now 1965 and the housing market is declining to the point where John and Pat have decided to close their California real estate office. The market was at that time somewhat like the 2009 market. Real estate sales were few and soon the office overhead was larger than the income. They needed to close that office to shut off the expense.

John told me:

We had been registered as Amway Distributors for several months, we heard success stories, we loved the products, Pat had customers but we had not yet decided to focus on building a large distributor organization. We were running out of money, and we could not get financing for our real estate customers. It was decision time and we decided to put all of our time and energy into the Amway business.

We knew that to make this a long term, successful business, our kids needed to know what was going on and we needed their support. The children did not have much to give up and knew the seriousness of the family financial situation. They wanted the family to survive and all five wanted to be of some help. Pat gathered the family around the kitchen table for a family conference.

By the time we decided to make this change, Pat had about 60 retail customers and had sponsored a couple of people who purchased products. Pat had a very full plate with five kids, little money and a business to run from our home. Pat loved the products and believed in their value. She became a very good manager and had the ability to convince others that the products were the best. She set aside a small room in our home as our Amway Office and set specific hours for distributors to get products.

At that time Amway did not deliver products. We drove to Norwalk Transfer and Storage to get products and distributors got their products from our home. As a family we had few options. We still had good credit but no money. We decided that we would spend full time building an Amway distributorship. We were both self confident that we could make a good living by owning a large Amway distributorship. Pat had some contacts with people who played bridge and John knew many of his competitors in the real estate business.

We had attended several meetings but couldn't get anyone to go with us. We knew the Amway business was a good business. We knew it was necessary to build a large distributor organization to do well but we couldn't grow the business by taking prospects to recruiting meetings. People just wouldn't go with us. I realized that we needed to build the business the old fashioned way: Take the business to the prospect.

The kids understood that we would be gone a lot and they would have to deal with babysitters. We were not well established in California and it was difficult to find babysitters who were dependable and capable of dealing with five children. Our oldest, Jo Ann, was about 12 or 13.

Late one night when we returned from holding a meeting, we paid the babysitter and took her home. When John arrived home from that delivery Jo Ann was still up and wanted to talk. She said that we should not be paying these sitters because she did all of their work and they did nothing. During meeting nights for the next several years Jo Ann was the person who took the leadership role in making sure the family was safe and cared for. She knew we had little money and would not take payment for her work. Her support gave us peace of mind and was a big factor in our success. Later on Jo Ann, David, Jill and Mary made the DD level and Susan helped when needed.

John decided to get out of the house in the morning and wander around Orange County meeting people and hopefully get them to like him. John would spend his time visiting people he had met through his real estate connections and invite them to look at the Amway opportunity. Though he was new to California, he had treated people with respect, and people liked him and trusted him. Most of the people he approached at least agreed to listen to him, and some of them decided to expand their economic prospects in this down market through joining John's Amway business. Sometimes it worked, and from this effort came hundreds of new friends and hundreds of distributors.

Pat's job now was to get more customers who would order the products. When they had first opened their Amway business, Pat was not thrilled with the idea of selling products, but after a while she found her own style. The women she had met were not always impressed with Pat wanting to sell them Amway products, and in their own little ways let Pat know. One of these women finally agreed that Pat could come over and 'show her what she had', so Pat brought over a few basic cleaning products, including the metal cleaner. Pat's friend had a coffee table with a copper top. Pat offered to demonstrate using the table. Her friend agreed.

Pat proceeded to clean one small portion of the table, and within moments it gleamed like it was new. Her friend was impressed, but obviously not ready to stoop to actually buying Pat's product. So Pat ended her demonstration with the table only partially clean, thanked her hostess, and left. Pat received a call a few days later with an order for metal cleaner and a few of the other products Pat had shown her.

John and Pat worked 24/7 for five months to earn enough to pay their minimum bills. They worked with motivated distributors to sponsor a sales organization. After about six months of aggressive selling and sponsoring they were earning enough to at least begin to stay even financially. The earnings started to increase as more people joined their group and within a few years their earnings were great.

John tells me their Amway business has provided a stable income for them every month since June 1965. "It has been our total business income for over 40 years. I am now in my 80s, and I am still operating the business because my wife and I enjoy keeping active in the business at a much slower pace. The business has enabled Pat and me to work together while raising our five children. They are now educated and own their own homes. We believe the Amway business provides a good lifestyle for people who like to have a business of their own."

CHAPTER 17

Daryl
Young and Single

℘

Quick Summary:

Daryl is a single 25-year old who has been away from his family and feels like he's on the outside looking in as everyone else has their family events. He realizes he may be single for awhile. He does not want to get married just to get married; he wants to find the right woman. He realizes he needs to create a life for himself that gives him a feeling of meaning, and from there he can more easily identify and attract the 'right woman'.

Daryl is **in the business of:** creating a life into which he can invite the right woman.

Exercise:

If this is you:

• Don't be in such a hurry to create a life that 'looks good' that you overlook what will sustain you over the long term.

• Give yourself time to get to know yourself as an individual in your new adult setting. Wait to make important commitments until you have enough experience with success that matters to you (as opposed to what you think others count as successful) so you have an inner knowing you're making the best decisions for you. This may end up being exactly what your parents think you need, or it may be a mix of their advice and what you learn on your own.

• Try to get past any sense of rebellion, and make choices only based on what feels best when you think of your future.

If this is someone you know:

• As much as you can, try to avoid giving advice.

• Of course you feel protective and you want the best for them. When you feel advice ready to come out of your mouth or you are ready to give that look, think about how much this advice is about you, and how much it's really likely to help this young person find their own inner wisdom and ability to cope with adult life on their own.

• Do what you can to provide unconditional emotional support, and practical support as needed, while showing confidence in their ability to make good choices for themselves.

℞

During dinner with his parents back at his childhood home, Daryl brings up the subject of life after college. He worked hard in college and his grades and the recommendations of his professors reflect this. His parents worked hard to cover his tuition and expenses, which he greatly appreciates. While he knows he has to live his own life, he wants to take into consideration whatever ideas his parents might have about his future, because he values the wisdom they've gained over their years of experience.

"We just want you to be happy," they tell him. "We are proud of what you have accomplished, and the next step is yours. We don't understand much about your professional field, so why don't you talk to some people who are successful in what you would like to do, and see what you can learn from them? Come back and talk with us about options if you like. Sometimes when you get out there and mingle with the people you want to be around anyway, interesting opportunities show up."

After dinner, while his mother does the dishes and his father reads the paper, Daryl takes some paper and a pencil and sits down at the living room table to sort out his thoughts.

He makes a list of his favorite classes in school, and writes down next to them what he liked about the classes. He makes a similar list of his professors, his extra-curricular activities, and the field trips, internships and other experiences he had and people he met during his college years. Then he thinks about his life before college, and writes down a few more.

He sits back and thinks about what matters to him. What does he most enjoy about life, and what really fascinates him about the future of the world, and his future in particular? He sets aside his written notes, and goes to bed with these questions in mind.

He wakes up with some ideas. Animals – raising children – a wife and partner who shares his interests – making a difference somehow in the world. He shares these thoughts with his parents at breakfast. "Better think about how to make a good living before you think about getting married," his father says. "Is there someone in the picture yet?" his mother asks. No, though he spent many lonely days at school wishing he had someone in his life, he had not yet felt compelled to develop any one relationship past a few dates and a friendship. "It's a good idea to make your own way first, anyway," his mother continues. "Create your own life and your own career, and then when you meet the right woman she will know what to expect from a life with you, and you will both have a better idea of whether or not you will be compatible over time in a practical way."

That made sense to Daryl. He sat down to review his notes from the previous night. He looked at the "what I liked about it" column, and found some interesting patterns. He liked to work with others when there was a strong team of intelligent, like-minded people who cared about the project at hand. He usually found himself in a position of leadership, though he did not seek it out. Other team members said they found him easy to get along with, and he seemed to understand what they were each talking about, so they trusted him to pull ideas together and make sense of the whole.

Beyond that, there was not any particular field or cause he was especially passionate about. He decided to start calling the people on his list, to ask for their suggestions and referrals. They were people he had trusted and enjoyed, and he hoped the people they knew would be similar.

This idea worked. He spent the next three weeks making new contacts and learning more about various fields and companies, and he began to hear about leadership opportunities that sounded interesting. Though he did not have enough experience yet to qualify for most of them, he did run into a manager who needed someone with his skill set right away. He was invited for an interview where he met the team he would be working with, along with his manager. Everyone seemed intelligent and interesting, and they made him an offer that day if he could start the next week. It was a good management position that came with a probationary period, which gave the company a chance to test out his actual abilities and his fit within the team and the company, and gave him a chance to see if the job was right for him.

It was a great start to Daryl's professional life, and he could see his future before him!

CHAPTER 18

Adolph Bolm
Second Chance & Lasting Legacy
ℰ

Quick Summary:

Adolph Bolm began life in advantageous circumstances. When it was time for him to begin school for his long term future, he failed miserably. Instead of fading into a failed life, he faced the exact same situation one more time, and this time he not only passed; he became a well-rounded student and he excelled. His brothers grew up and became successful in business, which was seen as safer and more lucrative than a career in the arts. By following his passion throughout his career, Mr. Bolm brought his knowledge, skill, pioneering spirit, integrity and compassion to his work, becoming a lifelong mentor and inspiration to his students, and leaving a lasting legacy for generations.

Adolph Bolm was **in the business of** mentoring and collaborating with artists, staging performances, and changing the face of dance.

Exercise:

If this is you:

• Think of this story if you have tried something and failed. If it's something that matters to you, think about what you can do different next time and consider giving yourself another chance.

• No matter where you start, it's always possible to build a legacy that gives meaning to people beyond your lifetime, especially when you follow what matters to you.

• As you move into increasing celebrity, focus on your message and your audience instead of letting external success puff up your ego.

• Kindness and integrity will keep you in your customers' hearts longer than anything else.

If this is someone you know:

• Respect them for what they have to contribute. Believe in them and their gifts.

• Try to understand their passion and encourage the value you sense in their vision, even if it is as yet underdeveloped.

• If they seem to fail, don't let them dwell on it. Help them focus on what they can do next. Ask them to consider giving themselves another chance.

၈၃

Adolph Bolm was born in St. Petersburg, Russia in 1884. His parents were in prominent positions in the arts, and he grew up with all the advantages of class and upbringing. He was admitted into the Imperial Ballet School at age ten and failed completely. He returned home and was so dejected that his parents implored the school to give him another chance, and this time he overcame and triumphed. He graduated in 1903 with first class honors in dance, music, painting and academic studies. His entrepreneurial spirit and innovations resulted not only in contributions that influenced dance and culture throughout the world, but also left a lasting impression on the people who knew him and worked with him personally.

During one point in his career he had his own studio, and other times he worked from some else's studio or theater. He worked by himself yet often brought in other teachers. He was always looking for a way to enrich his students, and enrich dance.

According to Rosalind de Mille, one of Mr. Bolm's dance students since she was ten, Adolph Bolm's 'own business' was "his heart, his knowledge, his curiosity and his spirit. It was what was within him, and he brought that to the places where he did his teaching. He helped me ... with my spirit!"

During a period in history when most people didn't travel much beyond whatever community they were born into, upon his graduation Mr. Bolm left St. Petersburg and made a tour of Western European museums and theaters. He was always interested in culture and the arts beyond the physical movements of ballet. He collaborated with other talented artists who were experimenting with new ideas. He organized his own dance company and tour in 1908, with fellow student Anna Pavlova as his partner, introducing her to the world outside of Russia.

As Adolph Bolm's international success grew, Sergei Diaghilev asked him to join forces with Ballets Russes instead of pursuing Bolm's own success. After some consideration Bolm agreed, joining Diaghilev as the principal character dancer in the first Paris season in 1909. Accustomed as the Paris audience was to more effeminate ballet styles by their leading male dancers at the time, he caused a sensation with his masculine power as Chief Warrior in The Polovtsian Dances from Prince Igor, causing the frenzied audience to tear off the orchestra rail of the Chatelet Theater. He led Diaghilev's company to America for their first two tours, and was called by The New York Times "the 'brains' of the Russian ballet in its American seasons".

Placed in a very difficult position because of his fellow dancer Nijinski's romantic liaison with Diaghilev and Nijinski's erratic behavior and jealousy for attention, Bolm was unable to leave the company because his solid reputation led Otto Kahn to threaten canceling the contract unless Bolm played an active role in the second American tour. Instead of quitting, Bolm worked harder and danced Nijinski's part when Nijinski was for some reason unavailable. During one of these times, the mattress that was supposed to cushion Bolm's fall in one part of the dance was mysteriously removed, and Mr. Bolm sustained a serious back injury. Instead of giving up, after he recovered Mr. Bolm decided to stay in America and start his own dance company.

Ever pushing the edges of convention, he was the first to introduce many ideas that eventually became modern and jazz style ballet. He was inspired by the American spirit, and saw in its youth, naïveté and mass culture the future of ballet. He settled in the United States and brought his new company, Ballet Intime, on a tour through the Midwest. "We are going to visit towns that heretofore have only been names to us. We shall cross the Mississippi. We shall see the high rugged mountains and the painted plains. We shall come to know America and America will come to know the spirit of the new dance," he said.

He continued to make his mark on American ballet, and also continued to appear internationally.

Always a pioneer, Adolph Bolm was at the forefront of moving pictures. In 1922 he recorded "Danse Macabre" in a short film, and demonstrated new dance moves that later became modern and jazz dance. He moved to Hollywood soon after, and to his disappointment found the ethics of the industry did not match very well with the morality of his upbringing. He reportedly missed some professional opportunities when he refused to provide ballerinas to some influential men in the industry. Similarly, being heterosexual in Diaghilev's company, though he was given charge of the company's American tour and danced Nijinski's part when Nijinski was otherwise occupied, Diaghilev's favors went to Nijinski.

Mr. Bolm had many ups and downs in his fortune. In addition to initially leaving his childhood ballet school in failure and despair, and breaking his back during the height of his career, he had two significant financial losses. He maintained his ties in Russia, sending most of his proceeds to a bank account there, losing everything during the Russian Revolution. Most of his family was able to escape and reunite in Riga. Later, a fire at his Hollywood home destroyed the remaining family treasures and valuables he had saved. Through it all, though challenging, he focused on what he loved and continued creating new ballet works.

Among other accomplishments during his American career, Adolph Bolm collaborated with John Alden Carpenter, Serge Prokofiev, Carlos Salzedo, Georges Barrere, Robert Edmond Jones, Nicholas Roerich, Michio Ito, Roshanara, Fedor Chaliapin, Igor Stravinsky, Nicolas Remisoff, Martha Graham, and Indra Devi among others. He was commissioned by the Library of Congress to choreograph the world's first performance of Apollo for their first ballet season. In 1932, he founded the San Francisco Opera Ballet, considered the oldest ballet company in America. He mentored Ruth Page, and taught ballet to Cyd Charisse, who at 14 began studying with him.

Wanting to create something essentially American, he created a jazz-pantomime to the comic strip Krazy Kat. Bolm said of this venture, "Here is whimsy that we seldom find in purposefully fantastic writing. If you seek subtlety there are fine meanings in Krazy Kat's amazing gestures. If you are blunt, there is hearty laughter in his incessant brick dodging".

Mr. Bolm was offered the post of ballet master of the Chicago Civic Opera in 1922, and Chicago Allied Arts in 1924. Ann Barzel, Chicago dance critic, wrote that his tenure produced "the greatest artistic splurge opera ballet has ever known." In 2003 Ann showed me a photo of Mr. Bolm with John Barrymore and told me with a twinkle in her eye, "We were all nuts about Adolph Bolm!"

Through all of this heady international success, he remained steady as a person. With one exception, everyone I have spoken with who knew him has only appreciation, respect and love for him, and feels moved to do whatever they can to document what he accomplished, and even more than that, who he was as a human being.

"He was wonderful," Rosalind said to me one day. "He had more integrity than anyone I have ever known since."

When I asked her how his integrity showed, she said, "Just in his breathing, just in his presence."

I've heard many stories about how he helped people throughout his life, and how he made decisions based on integrity rather than expedience, often giving up opportunities and publicity as a consequence.

Rosalind told me a story.

"When I was a young girl and we were doing Petrushka, we

were having a dress rehearsal. Everyone put on their costumes for the first time, and mine turned out to have a bag that came down from the naval down to the knees, down between my legs. Mr. Bolm saw that, and he thought I had something to do with this, and he pointed his finger and sent me out of the room in a rage, 'Out!'

I was embarrassed and humiliated beyond measure. But then he realized that I did not have anything to do with it, and he had the designer, well, fix it.

He took me on his lap in his arms and gently apologized, and comforted me. It was the costume that he was objecting to, not me, he told me."

"No wonder you loved him", I said to Rosalind.

"He was wonderful to me."

www.AdolphBolm.com

CHAPTER 19

Young Marilyn
Responsibility Without Authority

✍

Quick Summary:

This story is about me as a ten year old child living at home with my parents. I was the oldest of four children, and assumed a leadership role in my family which had dysfunctional characteristics. My brothers may have different memories; they were younger, they were boys, and different people. These are the events I remember, which I have corroborated with my parents' memories over the years.

My parents were all too eager to give me plenty of responsibility but no clear authority. My influence had to be channeled through activities deemed acceptable to my parents. There was little food, no heat, clean clothes were difficult to find, and there was emotional abuse and neglect. I took what I learned in school, from what I read, and my own reasoning to overcome obstacles to survival and finally find a way approved by my parents to begin living my own life. I had survival guilt and tried to offer my new life to my family, but they were not interested, and I realized everyone makes their own choices.

I was **in the business of** getting through childhood to have a future.

Exercise:

If this is you:

• Talk to yourself honestly and objectively about your situation. If this feels challenging share with someone you feel a safe connection.

• Address safety issues first. Write notes only if it is safe. If you feel threatened in any way, connect with someone who has authority to help you.

• Once you are safe, make a list of your current needs. Start with the basics: Did you get enough food to eat today? ... a place to sleep? Find something that helps you feel better ... take walk, notice the beauty around you, do something nice for someone else. Find comfort in things independent of your personal situation.

• Start with your most basic needs and move up Maslow's Hierarchy of Needs (see Needs Literacy page page 233) Create a plan to begin filling those needs, and start following your plan. Check in with yourself regularly to become better acquainted with your own needs. As you get better at identifying and meeting your own needs, translate that skill to understanding the needs of others.

• Bring to mind any dreams you have for improving your life. Start giving yourself little things that help you believe you are moving closer to having those dreams.

If this is someone you know:

• You may have a desire to move this person out of their situation into one that more closely matches the ideal you have in your mind for this person.

• Remind yourself that your ideal may not be that person's ideal situation, or that they may need to take small steps at first to improve their situation.

• Think about resources that could help this person, and, only if it's appropriate and with this person's permission, do what you can to help the person mobilize resources for themselves.

• Don't moralize or add to their burdens by dwelling on how bad things are. Help them focus on positive, incremental, attainable steps.

• Remember YOU are NOT responsible for THEIR situation, and you may or may not be able to help them fix it. Take stock of your own life and your own needs, and remember to live your own life and take good care of yourself.

• When you feel helpless, remember that's normal. You'll be better able to help them if you're getting support elsewhere. Remember it helps them just to know they have a friend who cares.

ℰↄ

As I begin my story: Marilyn is used to responsibility. Her parents have left her in charge of her younger brothers regularly, she's already been earning extra money through babysitting and working in the soybean fields, and she's spent her money buying a typewriter on layaway and seeds for the garden she maintains. Her mother buys food on Saturdays at the grocery store while her dad spends money in the bar as she and her brothers wait in the car which is parked in the grocery store parking lot. Sometimes there is not enough money for food, so the family relies on Marilyn's garden.

When it's not Saturday, her father is usually 'on the road' trying to sell life insurance, and her mother is usually in bed, depressed. When her mother gets up, she is a good cook, and Marilyn has learned by watching her. When her dad is home he is often fixing the car. Marilyn has learned by watching him, too, but he usually shoos her away because 'boys should be learning about cars, not girls.'

Marilyn is very resourceful. She finds her mother's cookbooks and tries out recipes based on the food that's available. Between the apple tree, garden tomatoes, beets, squash, onions, lettuce, radishes, corn, green beans … during summer there is plenty of food. Marilyn learns about canning food, so she begins to process the extra food for winter. Her mother gets interested and buys peaches they process together.

Marilyn is also used to hardship. The winters get very cold. During years past she has discovered if she brings her blanket to the living room and puts it over the grate that comes from the furnace, she can trap the heat and stay warm during the night. Though the heat would just go into the unused room, she has to sneak in quietly because Marilyn's mother will tell her to go back to bed if she catches her. But as the years go by the furnace no longer provides heat.

In school Marilyn learns about the pioneers, and she begins to check out books from the library about the pioneer days. The characters in the books are dealing with the same conditions she has: during blizzards it's difficult to see more than a few feet, so navigating around outside is perilous. The pioneers would gather around a fireplace or cast iron stove where they could burn wood to keep them warm, but this wasn't available in Marilyn's home. Marilyn's home was designed to be heated with heating oil, or propane for the kitchen stove, neither of which Marilyn could provide.

Marilyn finally read a story about a father who put stones on the hearth to warm them, then wrapped them in cloth and place them at the foot of his children's bed under the covers to warm the bed for them. Marilyn looked around her house for something she could use in this way. Because there was electricity and the water heater worked, there was always hot water. Her mother also had a hot water bottle. Marilyn found if she let the water run, then filled the water bottle with the hot water, it would stay warm under the covers until she got to sleep. This became her routine during the winters.

She sometimes thought about her brothers, and felt uncomfortable about having the only source of heat during the night, so she offered to share it with her brothers. None of them was interested.

She also learned in the pioneer books that they would close off unneeded rooms during the winter, because it was easier to heat a smaller space. The house Marilyn lived in was a large farmhouse, and was not suited to this kind of strategy. Again, Marilyn became inventive and arranged chairs in the living room in such a way that they formed a tent when blankets were placed over them. Marilyn got her brother's permission to use their blankets during the day, but again, they were unwilling to join her in her tent. Marilyn didn't understand, and wish they had contributed their body heat to her little structure, but she appreciated the use of their blankets.

She began to realize her brothers needed someone to turn to when there was conflict, and her parents were not available to fill this role. Marilyn learned about the judicial system in school, and told her brothers she was available to listen to both sides and come up with a solution when they could not solve their own problems. She was called upon several times, and the judicial ideas she had learned at school seemed to work.

As the years went by, her parents noticed she was more and more capable of taking on responsibility, and they gladly delegated more to her. They still maintained the power, and at odd times would decide to pull resources she needed to complete the task at hand. At 15 she was exhausted, and even though seventeen was the magic age she had been working toward when her parents said she could legally be on her own, she began to look for ways to leave home earlier.

She spoke with an attorney in town who said she could be considered legally emancipated because she had been earning her own living for some time. Marilyn did not have enough money saved to pay for an attorney, so she endured her situation a little longer.

Finally one day she had an unexpected break. Her mother had found a live-in babysitting job in the paper, helped Marilyn contact the family, took her to the interview in town, and gave her a good recommendation. The family hired Marilyn on the spot!

This not only changed Marilyn's location, but also her options. She learned there was a completely different way to live, where family fights were rare, and healthy food was plentiful. It was Marilyn's job to do the cooking and make the shopping lists. It took her awhile to learn she could put healthy, and even expensive, items on the shopping list and the items would appear, ready for her to use. The support was wonderful!

Marilyn was now living closer to the college, and began sitting in on lectures and activities there. She met new friends and learned more about what was possible in life. She learned to play the guitar, she decided she liked educational psychology, and she began volunteering at the hospital and a telephone youth emergency service. She took a job as a waitress, and then as a secretary at the local social services agency, where she learned how to help the poor get out of poverty. She learned her lessons well, and began a life of possibilities.

She met wonderful teachers and continues to learn. Her life is still getting better, and she is grateful every day because she knows what a wonderful life she has, even on the most difficult days!

CHAPTER 20

Rose, George and Brian
On Their Own

&

Quick Summary:

Brian was born in the early 1900s, and tells the story of how he and his brother and sister survived the depression without either parent available to help them. It's a story of dealing with circumstances as best they could, and finding ways to work together as a family. All three children grew up and had successful careers and families of their own.

Rose, George and Brian were **in the business of** growing up as normally as possible under the circumstances, and keeping their family together.

Exercise:

If this is you:

• Focus on the positive.

• Be realistic about your situation. Know there is a way through this.

• Think about your immediate situation, and set step by step goals for yourself to take care of your basic needs such as safety, food, shelter, clothing.

• If you fall short of your goals, remember it's only temporary. You have your whole life ahead of you, and plenty of time to grow up. The key is to understand, accept and learn as you progress. Just re-think your plans and make adjustments. That is what adults have to do. You are simply learning these skills a little earlier than usual.

If this is someone you know:

• Don't make assumptions. There is much wisdom and ability in the young and elderly, even though they have some dependency needs. Ask the person how you can help before you tell them what they need.

• If you are concerned for their safety, think realistically from their point of view first before intervening. Are they really unsafe, or are you projecting your own model of childhood onto their situation? If they are unsafe, do what you can to help them, without depriving them of their own self-determination.

• If there are ways you can help without taking over, respectfully provide support as you can. Remember everyone owns their own experience and it's an exquisite gift to find our way through challenges. It's so easy to take self-determination away from someone we see struggling, or who we label dependent or needy. Reach out and offer support, listen to them, try to understand them from their own point of view, and offer suggestions that help them maintain ownership of their own lives and choices. When you see them getting through things, acknowledge it and let them know how amazing their accomplishments are.

ℰↃ

Brian's father left the family the day Brian was born, leaving his three children Brian, George age one, Rose age two, and his wife. He never gave an explanation, and only returned on the day of Brian's graduation from college. Brian's mother, completely devastated by the experience, was admitted into a mental institution. The three children were sent to a nearby orphanage.

After living together for a few years, George and Rose were moved to an orphanage in another state, while Brian stayed in the orphanage closer to their home, which was becoming overcrowded. The new orphanage had better facilities for older children.

Mother Weinstein ran the orphanage, and took a special liking to Brian. He may have had a special place in her heart, but he still had to live with the other children.

"I had to make sure I ate my food quickly, because if you turned and talked to the guy next to you, your food would tend to disappear. This was a big, long table. You were very careful to not take your eye off the food. It was a way of living. When you are served food, you learned to eat it. You get hungry otherwise."

During the years the children were in different orphanages, Rose and George were determined to find a way to bring their family back together again. When Brian was eight, their grandmother agreed to help them, and found a family that was willing to take in Brian and George. Rose was sent to another family in the richer part of town. Brian's foster family could hardly afford the extra expense, but they managed for two years until 1929 when Mr. Miller lost his job and the family lost their home.

The Millers had three children, which Brian took care of when the parents were away. Brian was also assigned the job of washing the floor every Friday afternoon before Saturday night services started. Brian is now 90 years old, and to this day he knows it is his special job to keep the kitchen floor clean. He still takes pride as he tells you the story and sweeps up some fallen crumbs.

When the Millers lost their home in 1929, Brian and George went to live with their grandmother. She had her own problems. Her husband had done physical work, had become injured, and was now lame and couldn't work. She was already caring for Brian's two young uncles, Neil and Bob. Brian reminisces about the many hours he enjoyed listening to Neil and Bob playing the piano and singing. At an early age, the kids were out working. Bob earned extra money selling vegetables, and Brian helped him. "It was the first time I made a couple of dollars. I worked in the fruit and vegetable markets. I was ten and eleven, and making some pocket money. George was working in a filling station learning to be a mechanic."

This lasted a couple of years until Neil and Bob father died, which affected their grandmother's income. By then George was 14 and Rose 15. The two older children teamed up and decided to take a hand in raising their younger brother.

They found an apartment across the street from the library. Brian appreciated that, because he loved books. Rose found domestic work, and George worked as a mechanic. They both quit school and their whole goal was to make sure Brian didn't quit school. They gave Brian a very bad time whenever he found a small job and suggested he quit school to help out financially.

Brian was a conscientious child, and very interested in science. He excelled in his courses, and received some of the highest scores in his class. "I got through high school, did very well, and studied at the local university. I couldn't afford the street car fare, so I walked about five miles to and from school."

Brian met Jean when he was fairly young, living across from the library. Jean lived a couple of blocks away. Brian wasn't allowed to go out on many dates, because George and Rose wanted him to focus on his studies. Jean was patient, and their wedding was the day after Brian graduated from college. They were married on the synagogue steps, because they had no money to hire the facility. "They didn't charge me any money to use the steps. Mother Weinstein was a key person at the wedding."

Brian did very well in college. When he graduated, he took a job with a manufacturing plant in. "They put me in a training program, and I was shown a lot of preference; I was going to do great things for them. They were beginning to do work for the war. Then the war started and we were the first ones going into the Army because we didn't have families. I called my friend Jim. All through college I had known him. I called him and told him I was going into the army so he would know where to write me. His reaction was, "Don't you dare go into the army. I am at a university where something new is happening. I'm going to learn more about it. I know we need people with your skills, and I would like you to forget about the army and consider working with us."

Brian moved with his wife to the city. He made great progress at the company, working with top notch people. "We started right from the beginning doing research on new materials. No one talked about safeguards to protect people working with the materials, and it turned out some of those materials were extraordinarily toxic." Like his fellow workers, Brian contracted a rare disease from his work. "I am the only one left. Most of the others died early. It might have something to do with the fact I have always been very physically active."

Brian moved with the company when they built their new laboratories. "I was part of the building of it. I was the leader of the material science building, so we moved again to be near the plant."

Brian and Jean had three children, and raised them in their new home. Brian joined the Men's Garden Club and filled the bare land around their house with trees, shrubs, and food for the table. He showed me the right way to peel a tomato, reaching to pull a few tomatoes down from the window sills where they were waiting to ripen.

When I met Brian, I met his wife Georgia. Jean had suffered from diabetes, and after a long illness while Brian kept careful and loving watch, Jean died. Brian was lost, and found the dating experience highly unsatisfying. A mutual friend finally convinced Georgia, who had long since given up on the opposite sex, to go on a blind date to meet Brian. Brian and Georgia quickly fell in love and were married.

Brian talks about the importance of saving money. "We have been living a frugal life. If you put it away early enough and just leave it alone, even at a low interest rate, and it is put into things that will not fail, you will have a nice nest egg when you need it later in life."

Georgia lent her considerable artistic and architectural skills to the house, and it became uniquely theirs. They learned to dance together, and when Brian retired, they spent their days building flowerbeds and enjoying their lovely yard.

Tools & Resources

"When the student is ready, the teacher appears."

One of the secrets to my success is I have always had wonderful teachers. Initially they came through books I borrowed at the local library as a child. Through psychology and history books I learned about possibilities beyond the survival level of my current existence. The books about pioneers taught me actual strategies I used to deal with raw conditions of nature day to day.

This section is a simple catalog of tools that inform the way I work.

Shared knowledge brings us power.

Together we are more than the sum of our parts.

TOOLS & RESOURCES
My Mentors

Welcome to my notebook reflecting my journey learning from these wonderful leaders and great thinkers.

I am certainly not an expert in their subject matter, and I hope my notes are useful to you. I'm sharing an outline of the wisdom I've distilled from my time reading and studying their work, and conversations I have had with them personally. I never had the privilege of meeting Peter Drucker; the wisdom I present from him comes from my conversations with Marshall Goldsmith and Frances Hesselbein.

I hope you are inspired enough to find their books and read more of their work. I expect their wisdom can help all of us navigate through the tough times as well as times of plenty that often take us beyond our current pool of knowledge. Take these great people with you and you will always find a new idea to inspire you.

By the way, if it looks like I'm selling these's people's ideas, I am! I'm hoping this book will appeal to the many small business owners, their customers and stakeholders who do not have the same access to leadership development resources as larger corporations. I'm hoping my distilled versions of my mentor's messages will help busy small business owners with new ideas to help them manage this challenging time, and that more people learn about these very useful concepts offered by some of the greatest thinkers of our time.

Nathaniel Branden

Conscious Living:

• Indications of living unconsciously: living mechanically, responding to events automatically.

• Living consciously has its roots in respect for reality: a respect for facts and truth.

• Creating an environment in which facts are treated as facts, truth is respected, question-asking is valued and not punished, and conflicting messages are noticed and clarified, enhances safety.

• The more rapid the rate of change, the more dangerous it is to live mechanically. We have nothing to protect us but the clarity of our thinking.

The Six Pillars of Self-Esteem:
Self-esteem is a consequence of internally generated practices. We can address the source of our self-esteem by understanding the following practices and initiating them within ourselves, and dealing with others in such a way that we encourage them to do likewise.

• Living Consciously
• Self-Acceptance
• Self-Responsibility
• Self-Assertiveness
• Living Purposefully
• Personal Integrity

Self-Reliance and the Accountable Life:

Taking Responsibility talks about autonomy, freedom and responsibility, and self-reliance and self-responsibility in society, romantic love, and in organizations. It also discusses challenges in separation and accountability.

We are ultimately responsible for our own existence. No one else is here on earth to serve us, take care of us, or fill our needs. We own our lives and no one else's.

Taking responsibility to this extent means we are willing to generate the causes of the effects we want. Others are not responsible for giving us what we want. If we want something from others, we must provide them with meaningful reasons to help us in terms of their interests and needs.

Self-Esteem in Business:

The further we move from a culture of top-down management, the more important self-esteem is to give our people the tools they require to respond to the needs of our organizations. As work becomes more an expression of thought, resourcefulness becomes more important than obedience and reliability.

High self-esteem confers a competitive edge. It tends to inspire respect from others. If you have good self-esteem your communications are likely to be honest, open and appropriate, and you are more likely to be attracted to nourishing rather than toxic relationships. Leaders with high self-esteem are more likely to ask, "What needs to be done?" instead of "How do I avoid looking bad?"

For more information:

The Art of Living Consciously by Nathaniel Branden
Simon & Schuster
ISBN 978-0-684-83849-6

Self-Esteem at Work by Nathaniel Branden
Jossey-Bass
ISBN 0-7879-4001-1

The Six Pillars of Self-Esteem by Nathaniel Branden
Bantam
ISBN 0-553-37439-7

Taking Responsibility by Nathaniel Branden
Simon & Schuster
ISBN 0-684-83248-8

Chris Coffey

Soon after I met Marshall Goldsmith in 2002 Marshall introduced me to Chris Coffey and Frank Wagner, who were collaborating with him on a stakeholder-centered approach to executive coaching. I've enjoyed working with all three of them ever since!

Chris has a wonderfulbackground as a professional actor, which he brings with focus and exuberance to his seminars and keynote presentations along with his indepth knowledge of people and business.

In addition to providing Stakeholder Centered Coaching to senior executives, Chris offers a series of workshops he calls Leaders Levers:

The Excellent Manager
Strategic Selling
The DNA of Teams: DNA article
GEO Prometheus Leading in Fast Time
Influence without Authority
Leadership Styles for Influencing Others

The **After Action Review** Chris uses in his coaching:

What did you set out to do?
Why?

What actually happened?
Why did it happen?
What insights did you have?
What are you going to do moving forward?

For more information:

www.ChristopherCoffey.com

Peter Drucker

Peter Drucker's wisdom has come alive to me as two of my mentors, Marshall Goldsmith and Frances Hesselbein, share how he inspired them.

Self Assessment

According to *The Five Most Important Questions*, Peter Drucker says the following key questions are simple, yet complex and compelling. They can be used as a self-assessment tool in any organization. Peter Drucker says this tool was intentionally developed as a flexible resource. The self-assessment process calls for broad participation to ensure understanding, ownership, and readiness to act. A detailed Process Guide is available which shows how to properly organize and direct the self-assessment process.

> Question 1: **What is our mission?**
> Question 2: **Who is our customer?**
> Question 3: **What does the customer value?**
> Question 4: **What are our results?**
> Question 5: **What is our plan?**

Wisdom

"We teach leaders what to do. We do not teach leaders what to stop. Half the leaders I meet do not need to learn what to do. They need to learn what to stop."

"The leader of the past knew how to tell, the leader of the future will know how to ask." (Frances Hesselbein October 2008 in New York)

For more information:

The Five Most Important Questions You Will Ever Ask About Your Organization by Peter F. Drucker with Jim Collins, Philip Kotler, James Kouzes, Judith Rodin, V. Kasturi Rangan, and Frances Hesselbein
Leader to Leader Institute
ISBN 978-0470227565

Wokbook: Jossey-Bass ISBN 1-55542-595X

Marshall Goldsmith

Marshall Goldsmith is a world authority in helping successful leaders get even better – by achieving positive, lasting change in behavior: for themselves, their people and their teams.

FeedForward Exercise

Marshall created a Feed*Forward* exercise which involves asking key stakeholders to provide suggestions for the future that might help the client achieve a positive change in their selected behavior. No discussion of the past is allowed, and no attempt to defend or explain past perceptions is permitted. The client simply takes verbatim notes documenting the stakeholder's suggestions for the future, and the only acceptable response to suggestions is "Thank you!"

> ### Giving FeedForward:
> • Be honest and fair
> • Be a positive, supportive coach
> • Offer ideas for the future
>
> ### Receiving FeedForward:
> • Take careful notes of ideas
> • Suspend judgment and any need to defend or explain
> • Just say thank you!

Marshall Goldsmith's Coaching Method

In Marshall Goldsmith's FeedForward coaching method, each person being coached agrees to involve key stakeholders in their coaching process. The stakeholders are chosen by the person being coached (the client) with approval by their manager. The coach interviews each stakeholder, asking what the client is doing well, and what could be improved. The coach creates an anonymous list by topic of comments received, and presents this to the client. Assuming the client **accepts** these comments, **acknowledges** they can improve, and **commits** to changing behavior, the coach then helps the client choose one behavior to focus on for the year-long coaching engagement.

This means the client chooses their own behavioral goal and their key stakeholders. The coach screens stakeholders initially to assure they are willing to let go of the past and to become a positive coach for future improvement.

The coach teaches the client to **apologize** to everyone affected by their behavior (to erase negative baggage associated with prior actions), to **ask for help** in getting better, and to **advertise** their improvement efforts (because co-workers often don't notice this on their own).

The coach also helps stakeholders become positive coaches to the client, helps the client follow up on a regular basis through **monthly** 5-minute conversations between the client and stakeholders using **Feed*Forward*** and helps them apply ideas generated through the process.

The result is that an entire team enjoys the benefits of coaching. Stakeholders may choose a behavior to improve as well, so the 5-minute session can become a two-way FeedForward session.

A unique component of Marshall Goldsmith's coaching is a pay-for-results model. Periodic mini-surveys are sent to stakeholders to monitor progress toward the goal. The coach receives payment only when stakeholders determine the client has achieved measurable improvement in the target behavior.

20 Annoying Habits

In *What Got You Here Won't Get You There* (Hyperion), Marshall Goldsmith and Mark Reiter discuss twenty workplace habits successful people need to break:

1. Winning too much
2. Adding too much value
3. Passing judgment
4. Making destructive comments
5. Starting with "No," "But," or "However"
6. Telling the world how smart you are
7. Speaking when angry
8. Negativity, or "Let me explain why that will not work"
9. Withholding information
10. Failing to give proper recognition
11. Claiming credit that we do not deserve
12. Making excuses
13. Clinging to the past
14. Playing favorites
15. Refusing to express regret
16. Not listening
17. Failing to express gratitude
18. Punishing the messenger
19. Passing the buck
20. An excessive need to be 'me'

Influencing Up

One of Marshall Goldsmith's most popular webinars has been about the art of influencing up. He presents ten guidelines in his article "Effectively Influencing Decision Makers: Ensuring That Your Knowledge Makes a Difference", available online at www. MarshallGoldsmithLibrary.com.

The ten guidelines listed below are intended to help you do a better job of influencing decision makers. In some cases, these decision makers may be immediate or upper managers—in other cases they may be peers or cross-organizational colleagues. I hope that you find these suggestions useful as you convert your good ideas into meaningful action!

1. When presenting ideas to decision makers, realize that it is your responsibility to sell—not their responsibility to buy.

2. Focus on contribution to the larger good—not just the achievement of your objectives.

3. Strive to win the 'big battles'—do not waste your energy and 'psychological capital' on trivial points.

4. Present a realistic 'cost-benefit' analysis of your ideas—do not just sell benefits.

5. 'Challenge up' on issues involving ethics or integrity—never remain silent on ethics violations.

6. Realize that your upper managers are just as 'human' as you are—do not say, 'I am amazed that someone at this level...'

7. Treat upper managers with the same courtesy that you would treat partners or customers—do not be disrespectful.

Before speaking it is generally good to ask four questions:
- Will this comment help our company?
- Will this comment help our customers?
- Will this comment help the person that I am talking to?
- Will this comment help the person that I am talking about?

8. Support the final decision of the organization —do not say, 'They made me tell you' to direct reports.

9. Make a positive difference—do not just try to 'win' or 'be right'.

10. Focus on the future—'let go' of the past.

95 Year Old Man or Woman

You are about to receive advice from a very wise person. Listen very carefully to what this wise old person says.

First, take a deep breath. Take a deeper breath. Now, imagine you are 95 years old and you are just about to die. Here comes your last breath. But before you take your last breath, you are being given a wonderful gift: the ability to travel back in time and talk with the person reading this now. The 95-year-old you has been given the chance to help the you of today have a great life.

The 95-year-old you knows what was really important and what was not; what really mattered and what did not; what really counted and what did not count at all. What advice does the wise 'old you' have for the you reading this? Take your time. Jot down the answers on two levels: personal advice and professional advice. Once you've written these words, take them to heart.

For a complete list of books, articles, columns and videos by Marshall Goldsmith visit www.MarshallGoldsmithLibrary.com.

For more information:

The Leader of the Future 2 edited by Frances Hesselbein and
Marshall Goldsmith
Leader to Leader Institute
ISBN 978-0-7879-8667-4

*The Organization of the Future 2: Visions, Strategies, and Insights on
Managing in a New Era* edited by Frances Hesselbein and Marshall
Goldsmith
Jossey-Bass
ISBN 978-0470185452

Succession: Are You Ready? by Marshall Goldsmith
Harvard Business School Press
ISBN 978-1422118238

What Got You Here Won't Get You There by Marshall Goldsmith
with Mark Reiter
Hyperion
ISBN 978-1-4013-0130-9

*Mojo: How to Get It, How to Keep It, and How to Get it Back When
You Need It!* by Marshall Goldsmith
Hyperion
ISBN 978-1401323271

Paul Hersey

Situational Leadership

When you wish to communicate effectively with people and exert influence, knowing your audience is invaluable. Situational Leadership offers a model which is depicted in a simple diagram, and can be applied in myriad conditions and situations.

Situational Leadership describes leader behaviors in terms of relationship behavior and task behavior, and takes into account follower readiness to be self-directed.

Leader Behaviors

Style 1: **Telling** – provide specific instructions and closely supervise performance

Style 2: **Selling** – explain your decision and provide opportunity for clarification

Style 3: **Participating** – share ideas and facilitate in making decisions

Style 4: **Delegating** – turn over responsibilities for decisions and implementation

Follower Readiness

Readiness 1: Unable and unwilling or **insecure**

Readiness 2: Unable but willing or **confident**

Readiness 3: Able but unwilling or **insecure**

Readiness 4: Able and willing and **confident**

Applying Situational Leadership

"One of the biggest opportunities in my life was Situational Leadership with Paul Hersey, and it has changed my life."
- Chris Coffey

Chris was a single father for nine years, and he raised two kids. In his seminars he tells his audience he used Situational Leadership to raise his kids. "The task specific-ness and the desired result are key determiners of what style to use," he says.

Chris asks people how they want to work with him in his coaching.

- Would you like me to tell you what I would do?
- Would you like me to give you some suggestions?
- Would you like to bounce your ideas off me?
- Would you like to run with it and get back to me if you need help?

Chris Coffey

Keynote Speaker, Leadership Coach and Trainer
www.ChristopherCoffey.com

Types of Power

- **Coercive Power:** sanctions, punishment or consequences for not performing
- **Connection Power:** association of the leader with influential persons or organizations
- **Reward Power:** providing things that people would like to have
- **Legitimate Power:** title, role or position of the organization
- **Referent Power:** attractiveness of interacting with the leader
- **Information Power:** access to or possession of useful information
- **Expert Power:** relevant education, experience and expertise

Situational Leadership During Crises

In February 2009 I asked Paul Hersey if the current economic crisis affected the way people interact with each other in terms of Situational Leadership. He told me that people tend to go into Style 1 whenever there is a crisis, but in reality you still need to match where people are. If you don't, you pull people into a crisis mode even when there is not a crisis. It becomes a self-fulfilling prophecy.

He said we get in trouble when everyone acts on a survival basis. People begin to think, 'I am going to withhold from other people and undermine them, so they get the pink slip instead of me', unless the company looks ahead.

> "What companies can do is look at their real people assets, identify who can help them turn things around, so that when the economy improves, they are in good shape. Let those people know they are on board, so they can win together, rather than continuing this undermining and withholding.'
>
> 'If you offer early retirement with bonuses, you end up losing the good people with confidence and pride in their work who know they can find another position. The people in the lower levels of Maslow's Hierarchy hang in there and stay.'
> 'Leaders in a crisis are feeling the same pressure everyone is feeling. A common response is to say, 'Listen to me. I know what to do.' which is Style 1. I am a firm believer that you need to match your communication style to the performance level of your audience. That is how you come across being concerned and realistic. If you come in too hard, it

becomes a self-fulfilling prophecy. Fear will turn to hatred, and people will attempt to undermine and overthrow you.'

'It is all about matching. If you are not giving me behaviors that match my readiness level, if you are not taking care of the needs I have, if you are not moving from leader directed to self directed, you are not going to get more performance out of fewer people.'

'The problem is companies immediately cut their training budgets in a crisis, but in reality this is when you need training budgets because you need to do more with fewer people. You need to make that possible by creating the right kind of training."

Paul Hersey, from our conversation February 2009

I was lucky enough to attend a Situational Leadership course with Paul Hersey personally at their center in Escondido, California. I highly recommend their materials and training courses as a way to better understand the concepts.

For more information:

Leadership: A Behavioral Science Approach by Dr. Paul Hersey, Ron Campbell
ISBN 0-931619-09-2

Management of Organization Behavior by Paul H. Hersey, Kenneth H. Blanchard, and Dewey E. Johnson
Prentice Hall
ISBN: 978-0131441392

Center for Leadership Studies, Inc.
Escondido, California
www.situational.com

Frances Hesselbein

Listening

• Listening is an art that includes respect, appreciation, and listening very carefully to the spoken words and the unspoken messages.

• Listening is one of the most effective ways of learning what the customer values.

• Communication is not just saying something; it is being heard; it is a connection, and is most successful when circular.

• Listening to the whispers of our lives is critical or we miss many messages to our inner self, our body, our heart, our spirit.

Circles of Inclusion

Peter Drucker said the modern hierarchy evolved because when the corporations were just emerging in the 1870s, the only structure that worked was the Prussian army, so they adopted the hierarchy structure of putting people in boxes, up-down, top-bottom, superior-subordinate.

I told our organization, 'That is not the uniform we are wearing'. It was all a matter of gathering people around and talking about circular management: "managing in a world that is round."

• People are ready if you include them. Nobody wants to be in a box.

• It is theirs; not yours. It is not that 'I am the great oracle and I am bringing you this'. 'It is ours.'

• In a small group we ask... 'How do you think it would work?'

• In a larger group ... "Our team has worked on a structure we would like to present.' Then it becomes theirs.

Warrior Ethos

Military integrity that translates to business and civilian life: The U.S. Army "The Warrior Ethos":

> • I will always place the mission first.
> • I will never accept defeat.
> • I will never quit.
> • I will never leave a fallen comrade.

To build an effective organization, we will always place the mission first, and never accept defeat. If we have a project, we are not going to quit; we are going to make it work. We do not leave a fallen comrade; we are going to help.   Maybe we have someone on our team who needs a new kind of support; they will get it.

Peter Drucker always said the U.S. Army did the best job of developing leaders in our country, because they develop leaders from within.

Frances Hesselbein

(Frances Hesselbein October 2008 in New York)

For more information:

www.LeadertoLeader.org

Hesselbein on Leadership by Frances Hesselbein
Jossey-Bass
ISBN 978-0787963927

Arthur Samuel Joseph

Vocal coach to many very high profile professionals to whom public presentations is an integral part of their craft, Arthur does much more than help people 'speechify'. He invites students to look deep within themselves and give voice to their most real and compelling Self. Continuing to practice personally what he asks of his students, after more than 40 years of daily application of his principles, he's able to help his students find a quiet, reverent and peaceful foundation upon which to trust expression of their gifts. He treats his new students with much respect and patience, and has a wonderful way of treating everyone as a valued friend.

Stature and preparation are everything in the Vocal Awareness principles he teaches. His coaching method is built upon seven rituals:

> Thank You to My Source
> Love and Let Go
> Allow a Silent, Loving, Down-Through-My-Body
>   Conscious Loving Breath
> See the Nasal Edge and Arc of Sound
> Take My Time
> Pay Attention/Deeper Listening
> Be My Self

See page 30 for Arthur's description of Self. See his book *Vocal Power* for more information about stature and the rituals.

When I first met Arthur, it was on a telephone call. I'd actually been aware of something about my voice I wanted to improve for over ten years when I met Arthur, and I'd tried everything I could find to make this change in my voice over that ten years. Without having met me or being able to see me in person,

with a few verbal comments he solved the mystery by making
a few suggestions and that is now a former characteristic of my
voice!!

For more information:

Vocal Power by Arthur Samuel Joseph
Vocal Awareness Institute
ISBN 978-1-588-72064-1

www.vocalawareness.com

Gary Ranker

Political Analysis

How do you navigate the waters of human relationships at work? Gary Ranker and his colleague Kathy McNay developed a political analysis tool that I find very useful. Contact Gary for a full explanation of how it is used. Following is a general description:

• Consider your key business relationships, how you feel after interacting with this person, and how much impact they have on you.

• Look for patterns to help you understand their support or lack thereof.

• Think about your goals, and how much each person is helping you or deterring you from achieving your goals.

• Prioritize which persons are most critical to helping you achieve your goals.

• Weigh the relative difficulty and payoff of change if you were to get persuade person to be more supportive of you attaining your goals.

• Create an action plan to facilitate each key person to be more supportive of you and your goals.

• Commit to dates by which you will have completed the agreed upon actions in your plan.

• Monitor periodically to stay on track with your action plan.

For more information:

Political Analysis Tool available at www.GaryRanker.com

Political Dilemmas at Work by Gary Ranker, Colin Gautrey, M. Phipps, Wiley ISBN 978-0-470-27040-0

Srikumar S. Rao

Meeting Professor Rao is an experience. Instead of saying 'have a nice day' you might hear him ask you, 'Will you commit to having an incredibly wonderful day?' Continuing the conversation with Srikumar, I've heard him say,

"I would like you to be open to the possibility that the ideas I share with you are going to profoundly change your life. What I do is I help highly intelligent, deeply driven, fiercely ambitious persons find deep meaning. The vision I have for you is that when you get up in the morning, your blood is singing for who you are and what you do. That as you go through your day, there are times you become radiantly alive.'

'That you have a deep sense of purpose, knowing you are doing exactly what you were put on earth to do. And you literally go down on your knees in tremendous gratitude and say 'thank you' for the good fortune that's been bestowed upon you. That you would pay for the privilege of doing what you do, and would gladly do it even if you weren't getting paid.'

'I'm talking about something much deeper than liking your job. I'm talking about where you're completely suffused with a sense of wellbeing and have an inner attitude of "Yes!" You feel what the poet speaks about, "God is in his heaven and all is right with the world."'

'I don't have to tell you that's rare, and that outside circumstances are kind of conspiring against you. If you're doing what you do just to get a paycheck, you're in very a sorry state.'

'What I'm talking about isn't a pipe dream. I'm submitting to you that a life like this can be yours, and what

I'd like to accomplish is to help you determine that you are not going to settle for anything less."

Professor Srikumar Rao
Author of *Are You Ready to Succeed?*, *Happiness at Work* and *The Personal Mastery Program*

As I finish writing this book Recession or Plenty: 7 Steps to Success in Business & in Life, I'm attending his 3-month course "Creativity and Personal Mastery". I thought with this kind of outlook, Professor Rao would be the kind of person I'd like to spend more time with as the financial markets search for stability, while more people lose their accustomed livelihood and begin to experience more anxiety, tension, uncertainty and fear. How does he maintain his attitude during the ups and downs?

Srikumar tells me that it's not so much what people around you are experiencing: It's more what you're sending out. If you're not on guard, the negativity around you can take over your life and smother you. He said we often think other people are doing things to us, when actually if we look at the thoughts we harbor, there is a close resemblance between our thoughts and what shows up in our lives.

I've been watching my own life and so far his assertion has been accurate. When I'm looking at the world and its many possibilities, more opportunities come to me. One winter day when I was feeling a bit down, I was frustrated with what I thought other people were doing to make my life more difficult, and I was focusing on what that meant to me. That same day I lost my wonderful, warm, expensive gloves. Maybe it was coincidence, but it seems odd to me that the only day I lost anything was the day I was focusing on how life was difficult and how much I was losing and it was someone else's fault.

For more information:

Happiness at Work by Srikumar S. Rao
McGraw-Hill
ISBN 978-007-166432-5

Are You Ready to Succeed? by Srikumar S. Rao
Hyperion
ISBN 1-4013-0193-2

The Personal Mastery Program by Srikumar S. Rao
Discovering Passion and Purpose in Your Life and Work
Sounds True Audio Learning Course

Ken Shelton

Ken Shelton plays a leading role in education for the business community though his books and his publications at Executive Excellence. As the primary editor for *7 Habits of Highly Effective People* by Stephen Covey, Ken spent several years refining concepts before the final draft was finally printed. Leadership authenticity and integrity are topics which underly all of Ken's work.

In his book *Beyond Counterfeit Leadership*, Ken talks about the entrepreneurial spirit and authenticity. He suggests the age-old questions 'Where did I come from?' 'Why am I here?' and 'Where am I going?' relate not only to the purpose and meaning of life but also to the meaning of every job.

Ken currently edits several quality periodicals which have become a mainstay among companies interested in improving leadership skills within their organizations. Recent columnists include: Barack Obama, Bill George, Carly Fiorina, Dave Ulrich, David Allen, Gary Hamel, George W. Bush, Gifford and Elizabeth Pinchot, Glenn Close, Harrison Owen, Jeff Immelt, Jim Collins, Jim Kouzes, Jim Rohn, John McCain, Ken Blanchard, Kevin Cashman, Lance Secretan, Malcolm Gladwell, Marcus Buckingham, Margaret Wheatley, Marianne Williamson, Marshall Goldsmith, Michelle Obama, Noel Tichy, Peter Block, Ram Charan, Richard Leider, Rosabeth Moss Kanter, Sally Helgesen, Stephen R. Covey, Tom Peters, Warren Bennis.

For more information:

Leadership Excellence Magazine
Personal Excellence Magazine
Sales and Service Excellence Magazine
www.leaderexcel.com

Personal Management Tools

Coaching

Coaching as an industry has grown tremendously over the past decade, both in the number of companies hiring coaches for their senior management, and also in the range of coaching specialties offered by the growing number of coaches available for hire.

A coaching investment is not just about a line item in your budget with funds there for a coach. A coaching engagement takes more than money. It takes time. and agreement with your coach regarding how you will work with each other. It takes a goal. It takes consistency. It takes trying new things.

Can you identify a behavior that limits you, where a positive change would improve your life? Do you care enough to make an effort to change?

This is the foundation of being coachable. If you are not interested in changing, this is not the process for you. If you are, a coach can make the difference between years of saying 'I should do something about this' to 'Well, that wasn't so difficult! What's next?!'

If you are the person being coached, why would you make that investment? Is it because your boss expects you to work with a coach? Is it because you want to get better at something? Is it because you have a feeling you are about to be fired or divorced so you think you have to get better or else …?

Whatever your reason, your time and attention are extremely valuable. How can you get the most return on your investment of time and attention?

First notice what gets in the way of you being coachable.

• Do you need to be the expert, know all the answers, be right all the time?

• Are you worried that you will lose your ability to make your own decisions if you take on a coach?

• Do you resist accountability?

• Do you expect coaching to be an onslaught of criticism and judgment about what you are doing wrong?

• Are you generally at odds with life, constantly defending yourself?

• Do you think that at your level of success, no one is qualified to give you accurate coaching?

I admit, depending on your coach, some of your concerns may be valid. With the right coach, it's worth getting past those mindsets because the results of overcoming a habit that gets in the way of further success in business and life is truly worth the investment. I say that from personal experience.

How to Choose a Coach

Everyone has their area of expertise, and this includes coaches. While I can help you improve behaviors, I hope you ask someone else to help you become a better football player, or run your accounting program.

You may choose a coach you get along with, or one you know will draw performance from you even if it's uncomfortable.

Marshall Goldsmith is the toughest coach I know. I've had the privilege of working closely with him for several years, which means, among other things, he has had the opportunity to see more of my flaws. He does not mince words. He gets right to the point. He is very direct. I have a picture in my mind of me standing next to him while he is extending his arm, pointing to a chair behind me, telling me to go and sit down until I had a better answer.

And how did I feel in that moment? I appreciated the clarity of his message, and I appreciated that he was not going to accept my weasely answer that positioned me less than who I could be.

From the outside it may have looked like a rebuke and punishment. From the inside it felt like support and encouragement. Why the difference? I felt no judgment from Marshall—only a clear message that he expected me to improve to the level I'd indicated I wanted to achieve. Stunning. No wonder he is in such high demand by so many top level CEO's and business leaders.

I have never felt Marshall's judgment or criticism. He has always treated me with the respect of a peer. Am I Marshall's peer? As a human being, of course I am. In the field of coaching, he is at a completely different level than me. Still he treats me like a human being. He treats me with respect. He can say anything to me from that frame of reference, and I won't hear that I've done something wrong. I will just hear his ideas as a gift for my consideration. My response: Thank you!

How to Choose a Goal

Look at your values, what your boss wants, what your stakeholders want, what will help you most in your work, how it fits at home, and choose a goal that you feel very good about. Something that will motivate you over the long term, or one day when you don't feel like following up.

Assessments

The good news: there are many assessments available. The bad news: we can tend to label ourselves with static ideas about who we are when we see the results of assessments about us. Use any assessment results only as a tool for looking at yourself in a new way. Judgments of others or ourselves rarely help. Focus on the positive! You are an evolving human being, with a great capacity to become a better new you! What ideas do you have for yourself for your future improvement?! Your assessment of yourself is as valid as any outside view of you. One may be more accurate than another, and each has some truth and value.

What's Next?

Marshall Goldsmith and Howard Morgan wrote an article about the importance of following up ("Leadership is a Contact Sport", strategy+business, issue 36). In their extensive study, they found that follow-up was the most important factor in behavioral improvement. Some methods of follow-up coaching:

• One-on-one coach
• Team coach
• Peer coach

Peer Coaching

In Peer Coaching, each participant acts as both the coach and the client. Each chooses a behavior to improve, and they meet regularly for support.

When senior management have experienced our FeedForward approach to coaching personally, they may want to expand the process to their entire organization. Peer coaching is a cost-effective way to implement a coaching initiative which allows more people within the organization to enjoy the benefits of coaching.

Our model of implementation has been:

• Participants complete some form of assessment. Find inexpensive online assessments at www.CoachMarilyn.com.

• Group seminar introducing the principles of Marshall Goldsmith's FeedForward coaching method, with an exercise to practice FeedForward and peer coaching with each other.

• Each participant is paired with a peer coach.

• Each participant chooses a behavior to improve, referencing assessment results as needed.
• Peer coaches decide among themselves how often they will check in with each other (daily or weekly), and how they will connect (in person, by phone or email). This is intended to be a 5-minute session.

• We provide follow up support to the organization as needed.

Two Peer Coaching Approaches

• Marshall Goldsmith FeedForward Exercise (page 152).
• Daily Questions

Daily Questions

• Make a manageable list of behaviors you would like to improve.

• Write each one as a question that can be answered either yes/no, or with a number.

• Decide with your peer coach how often you will check in, and the most convenient time.

The Daily Questions approach involves each person making a list of behaviors they would like to improve, and sharing the list with their peer coach. Each item on the list is written in such a way that it can be answered using 'yes', 'no', or with a number. Example: 'How many minutes did you spend exercising today?' During the 5-minute check-in, each coach reads the list for the other to answer. If the peer coaching sessions are weekly, this means each person will ask themselves their own questions each day, and provide the weekly total to their peer coach during the check-in session. When Marshall Goldsmith introduced this to me, he and his peer coach Jim Moore had a 5-minute call every day.

    If you want to track your progress, each coach can keep a spreadsheet with their peer coach's responses, and send the results to each other after a week or month, depending on the frequency of check-in sessions.

Coaching Etiquette

• Be respectful of each others' time
• Follow through on your promises
• Say thank you

Personal Goals or Company Goals

Some behavioral improvement goals span both personal and professional arenas. Some may be very personal. If your peer coach is a co-worker and you don't want to advertise your personal goal at work, you may want to establish a peer coaching relationship with a friend to get support for your personal goals.

Keys to Success:

• Be consistent.

• Keep the length of your behavioral improvement list to something that motivates you, and doesn't feel overwhelming.

• Remember, you don't have to do everything on your list, and you don't have to do it perfectly. If you think you do, then please add to your list, "How many times today did I take a deep breath and allow myself and others to be human?"!

• If you find yourself falling short of the same goal consistently, don't just assume you are doing something wrong. Take a moment to ask yourself how important this task really is to you. Is it the right goal? The right time? Removing the item or adjusting it may make it a more effective goal for you.

• Also remember you don't have to implement every suggestion you receive through FeedForward. Enjoy the myriad ideas you write down as you are receiving FeedForward, implement the one(s) that make sense to you now, and tuck the rest away in your treasure chest for the future.

• Be respectful of each other's time. Don't just call your peer coach and launch into a 20-minute description of your issues before they have had a chance to say if it's a good time for them. Stay honest with each other about what is working in your relationship, and what is not. If you are sincerely distressed by difficulties working with your peer coach, write down specifically what is not working (keep the list in case it helps you look at yourself through future relationships), and ask the person in your organization who manages the peer coaching initiative if you can be assigned a new peer coach.

Creativity

Creativity During a Recession

I spoke with Bob Thurman about current changes in the marketplace, and his thoughts on how to approach this turn of events:

> "You are really going to need creativity in the new world of business. New business models will be based on finding what other people need, and being of real service to people.'

> 'How to get mastery and creativity? Think critically. Think realistically.'

> 'First, become aware of what in your thinking and your mind is not you. Take time to be quiet with yourself, and notice your thoughts. Then notice the voice in your head who would speak those thoughts. As you become more aware, you can begin to choose which thoughts to listen to. Then you will no longer reactively take action on every thought, or keep thinking or even believing every thought. You will start to feel a sense of freedom.'

> 'And don't limit yourself by placing labels on the outward appearance of success you think you should achieve. That kind of conditioned thinking is just too limiting. You are capable of much more than you know. We are all really a work in progress.'

'Next, instead of focusing just on yourself and what you want, become very interested in other people's happiness. "You will begin to see how you and others are interwoven. You will come up with new business ideas based on what people need and want. This is how you can succeed in the new economy."

Robert A. Thurman (in a conversation March 2009 in New York), Jey Tsong Kappa Professor of Indo-Tibetan Studies Columbia University, personal student of His Holiness the Dalai Lama

Srikumar S. Rao has a similar point of view:

"While creativity is always highly valuable, it is especially important in the down times.'

'What happens in bad times is you are more constrained because your revenues are lower and resources are scarce, while at the same time new customers are fleeting, more difficult to find and more demanding.'

'In order to achieve superlative results you have to do things differently, and that is where creativity comes in. In fact, very often the only way you are going to survive is by being creative.'

'One of the best ways to be creative is to get out of the mindset of "What do I want?", and begin thinking from the perspective of "What do my customers want?"'

'Follow that up with ideas about "How can
I possibly give it to them given my current
constraints?" If you have that in the front of your
mind always, then things start happening."'

Meeting Professor Rao is an experience. Instead of saying 'have a
nice day' you might hear him ask you, 'Will you commit to having
an incredibly wonderful day?' Continuing the conversation with
Srikumar, I've heard him say,

"I would like you to be open to the possibility that
the ideas I share with you are going to profoundly
change your life. What I do is I help highly
intelligent, deeply driven, fiercely ambitious persons
find deep meaning. The vision I have for you is
that when you get up in the morning, your blood
is singing for who you are and what you do. That
as you go through your day, there are times you
become radiantly alive.'

'That you have a deep sense of purpose, knowing
you are doing exactly what you were put on earth
to do. And you literally go down on your knees
in tremendous gratitude and say 'thank you' for
the good fortune that's been bestowed upon you.
That you would pay for the privilege of doing what
you do, and would gladly do it even if you weren't
getting paid.'

'I'm talking about something much deeper than
liking your job. I'm talking about where you're
completely suffused with a sense of wellbeing and
have an inner attitude of "Yes!" You feel what the

poet speaks about, "God is in his heaven and all is right with the world.'"

'I don't have to tell you that's rare, and that outside circumstances are kind of conspiring against you. If you're doing what you do just to get a paycheck, you're in very a sorry state.'

'What I'm talking about isn't a pipe dream. I'm submitting to you that a life like this can be yours, and what I'd like to accomplish is to help you determine that you are not going to settle for anything less."

Professor Srikumar Rao

For more information:

Are You Ready to Succeed? by Srikumar S. Rao
Hyperion
ISBN 1-4013-0193-2

The Personal Mastery Program by Srikumar S. Rao

Discovering Passion and Purpose in Your Life and Work by Srikumar S. Rao
Sounds True Audio Learning Course

Daily Routine

I'd like you to come up with your own personal daily routine that supports your way of doing things. In the meantime, you can borrow mine, which I outline below. Even if you don't have time to do anything else toward your new goals today, at least take five minutes in the morning and five minutes at night to try this:

Morning

• Before getting out of bed, take a moment to welcome the new day.

• Remember your vision, and take a moment to see and feel how it will be when you are living the successful outcome of your vision.

• Thank (God, the Universe, your Higher Self, as you choose) for the wonderful people who will touch your life today, and ask that your interaction with everyone be a blessing to them and to you.

• Thank (God, the Universe, your Higher Self, as you choose) for the successful outcome of your goals today, and become open to learning something new through unexpected opportunities that bring you even closer to your highest good.

• As you wake up, look at your list of things to do, and imagine everything going smoothly and easily to get you closer to your vision.

Evening
Just before going to sleep:

• Say this to yourself (attributed to Ralph Waldo Emerson): "Finish each day and be done with it. You have done what you could. Some blunders and absurdities no doubt crept in; forget them as soon as you can. Tomorrow is a new day; begin it well and serenely."

• Let go of any lingering feeling of discomfort in mind, body or spirit, and go to sleep with a feeling of gratitude, focusing your imagination on what you want.

I know that going from a feeling of stress or argument to manufacturing a feeling of gratitude may seem farfetched, but I recommend you cultivate this ability. You don't have to be grateful for the way things are, but I have found real magic in being grateful in the midst of the mess. You are in the middle of something you don't like and apparently can't get out of in the moment anyway, so why not do what you can about it ... change your attitude and at least become more comfortable. I'm not exaggerating when I say that I have had amazingly positive experiences using this technique in situations that from the outside looked certain to be unhappy.

Your To Do List
Now, what do you put on your list of things to do today?

1. Mind Dump & Says Who
I know you have many obligations to many others, including family, job, maintaining your residence, taking care of yourself. You probably don't even remember all of the things you do. Do a mind-dump. Write them all down. If you can, list them in a spreadsheet, and in the column to the left of the list of items, put

the name of the person or organization you are doing this for. If you are sure you are doing something just for yourself, then put your own name down.

2. Now Do a Best-Case Scenario

Pretend you have all the time, health, money and opportunity in the world and make a list of all the things you really want to do. Everything you can think of, from eating ice cream for dinner to taking a cruise around the world. You don't have to do everything on your list. It does feel good to honor yourself enough to acknowledge your desires and put those on the list along with taking out the garbage and making your bed.

3. Vision

Does every item on your list have a person or organization or goal in the column to the left of it? Create another column on the left and think again about your vision that gets your juices going every morning. Put a number or a word in that column for each item indicating how closely that task aligns with your vision. This is more of a feeling exercise than an intellectual exercise, because your filters are probably geared more toward what you've always done in the past than what is possible in the future. You can always go back and change things later. For now just take your first gut reaction.

4. Priority

You knew this was coming. Make one more column to the left and put a priority on each one: A is most important, D least important, and Z something you don't want to even think about for now. You can add A1, A2, D3, etc., whatever makes sense to you. Create a key if it helps you remember later what you had in mind.

What it Means

This all just gives you good food for thought. In a spreadsheet you can sort by any column.

Sort by the "Priority" column and then look at the "Vision" and "Says Who" columns. Are some people or organizations in your life already more closely aligned with your vision?

Just take some time to look over your list from different points of view, and see what you can learn about yourself and your life.

You might feel very motivated and ready to make a big personal improvement list. I'll be happy if you just choose one or two things to improve. Here is what Marshall Goldsmith tells his clients to ask themselves:

"What am I willing to change now? Not in a few months. Not when I get caught up. Now. Then get started on the activity within two weeks, or take it off the list. And quit tormenting yourself!"

Marshall Goldsmith, Best-selling uthor
What Got You Here Won't Get You There
www.MarshallGoldsmithLibrary.com

Environment

What is the quality of your environments, and how well do they support you? Depending on the facet of your life or business you are focusing on, several environments may come into play. Use this random list of environments to help you plan projects, set goals, identify needs and resources:

Money

Strategic network

Physical location
Physical body and health

Relationships, family, social
Friends: male and female

Self image, self concept
Quiet time with self

Spiritual, nature

Learning, exploration, intellectual
emotional freedom and support

Community
Play, leisure

See Nathaniel Branden's description of how to create an environment of safety (page 146).

Financial Tips

Consult your CPA or financial advisor for specifics which relate to your industry.

The basics are simple:

1. Earn more than you spend.
2. Save what you can.
3. Use a budget.

If you're thinking about going into business, I recommend starting as lean as possible. Do you really have to lease that fancy office space and hire a full time receptionist? What can you do with no overhead at all? Can you start by just cultivating relationships with prospective customers and providing a service which costs little but your time?

Can you start by trying out different ideas while still enjoying a stabilizing income from your current source of revenue? Unless you have no other source of income and this is your only option, giving up your current source of security may be unnecessarily putting yourself at the edge of terror. Building a business takes confidence and focus. This is not the time to increase unnecessary challenges.

When asked to define a successful Amway business, Jay Van Andel, co-founder of Amway, is reported to say, "One that is profitable."

In a conversation between John Travolta and Larry King on The Larry King Show in 2008, John Travolta said he uses a budget. When Larry asked him, "Even you?" John replied, "If you want to keep any money, you have to budget. Anybody could lose what they make if they don't budget."

For more information:

Your Money or Your Life: Transforming Your Relationship with Money and Achieving Financial Independence by Vicki Robin, Joe Dominguez, and Monique Tilford
Penguin ISBN 978-0143115762

Finding Your Desk

How important is organization? I've been coaching small business owners for years on organizational principles from keeping track of those floating pieces of paper with phone numbers and appointments on them, to filing systems that work for both actuaries and sales people and procedures to streamline the paper flow in a business.

You might think that means my own office is spotless, with everything in its place. Although that is something I would enjoy, I also value the creative process, which can get very messy. To quote my friend David Lober: "What comes out of a workshop is more important than the condition of the workshop."

When paper comes in, I have one pile for important information I need to keep over time, a pile for things to do in the near future, and another pile for things I want to keep but don't have time to file yet. When it takes me longer to find a piece of paper than it should, that is when I know it's worth taking time to organize the pile.

Not everyone can think in a messy or chaotic environment. Not everyone can think in a spotless, sterile environment. Know what works for you, and create an environment that supports you and your process.

In case you are ready to create a filing system for your home office, here is a basic outline to start with:

Information (A-Z storage files)

1) Take 26 file folders (I get third cut without reinforced tabs, because I go through a lot of file folders.

2) Write a letter from A – Z on each folder tab.

3) Put them in a file drawer or box.

4) Keep some blank file folders nearby.

5) When you bring home some papers you want to keep for awhile, label a blank file folder, put the papers in the folder, and place the folder in alphabetical order. Simple.

6) Once a year or so, go through the folders to see if there is anything you can throw away or file in last year's archive.

Categorize

Here are some general categories you could use:

Personal
• Car
• Finances
• Health
• House
• School
• Shopping (this can help you save time and gas on errands)

Business
- Accounting
- Brochures
- Contacts
- Customers
- Events
- Goals
- Resource Material

Action Items (Hot Files)
- Bills to Pay
- Correspondence to Do
- Orders to Fill
- People to Call
- Read (keep this small unless you have a lot of time to read)
- Tickle (holding for more information, future events, etc.)
- To Do This Week (review this once a week)

See "How to Use a Planner" (page 203) for more information on getting organized.

Focus Session

What do very successful people report most often as their secret to success? "Focus!"

     Before I go to bed at night, and after I wake up in the morning, I do a Focus Session with myself.

• I sit down in a quiet place with my planner and look at my values and goals, and allow myself to feel what I will experience when I actually achieve those goals.

• Then I look at what I have planned for the upcoming day, and see how closely they are aligned with my values and overall goals.

• Is everything I'm planning to do actually addressing my needs, or have I taken on responsibilities that are not mine?

• What can I add to my day to inspire me and keep me happy?

• All of this takes about five minutes. I do this again throughout the day as I have time.

See the "Values-Based Time Management" section (page 218) for more information on discovering your values.

Healthy Exercises

If you consider there's only one of you, and your income and business rely on your ability to perform, hopefully you'll be motivated to give premium attention to your most important physical asset: your body.

I have often wondered why something so important has become a chore rather than a pleasure. Maybe it goes back to our teenage years when it was cool to smoke, drink, drive fast cars and try risky sexual exploits. It was not cool to take good care of ourselves, eat healthy food, floss our teeth, and maintain the clear head we needed to manage an already challenging transition in our lives. For those lucky enough to survive reckless experimentation without lifelong addictions or crippling disabilities, we still seem to carry habits we might do better without.

Personally I'm changing my own internal paradigms as I become aware of bad habits of thought and action, to paradigms and habits that support my health and make better use of my resources. Following is a list of new habits I've collected that might be helpful to you:

Morning

• Brush and floss teeth (did you know gum disease has been linked to heart issues, and that flossing even occasionally can help prevent gum disease?)

• Lie on the floor and do some exercises to start the day to help brain and body work together.

• Eat a healthy breakfast with protein within an hour of waking up.

• Take food supplements as needed to get complete nutrition for the day.

During the Day

• Walk, go up and down stairs, park on the far side of the parking lot, take every opportunity to get exercise.

• When reading or at the computer where eyes are at a fixed distance for long periods of time, get up at least every half hour and walk around. Look up at least every ten minutes and look at varying distances closer and farther away than the fixed computer or reading distance.

• When picking up something heavy, either get help, or use legs to lift rather than back to bear the weight. If possible, take it apart and move it in pieces, one piece at a time.

• Go to the gym as possible and follow a regular exercise plan to improve strength, flexibility and endurance.

• Drink plenty of water.

• Eat a healthy lunch that contains protein.

Before Going to Bed

• Make a list or journal or sort out anything stressful before going to sleep, so it doesn't affect resting time.

• Avoid eating two to three hours before going to bed.

• Turn off the TV and listen to some soothing music and read something uplifting and positive before turning off the light.

When Traveling

• Drink plenty of water.

• Have clothes and accessories that match the climate and weather.

• Bring healthy snacks, including protein snacks.

• Take extra food supplements as needed.

• Do Feldenkrais exercises when sitting for long periods of time.

When Stressed

• Take a deep, silent, conscious loving breath.

• Focus on what I want, instead of any bothersome thoughts.

I asked Arthur Joseph's advice one difficult period in my life when a series of losses finally penetrated my 'I can get through this' veneer. Feelings were beginning to surge over the levee, and I needed a way to focus. Arthur became quiet for a moment, and then suggested I try focusing on allowing a conscious loving breath.

This sounded very simple. I could remember the instructions. He did not say 'take' a deep breath, he said 'allow a conscious loving breath'. This took a little practice, especially when I was busy trying to hold back my feelings ... from whom? Mostly from myself. The breath took me through the levees I'd built up to and through the feelings, I started to relax, and life began to look reasonable again, despite current circumstances.

Taking Exercise to the Next Level

One of the healthiest exercises I know is called 'gratitude'. That may sound schlocky and pollyannaish, but I've found it to be very powerful, especially in situations least suited to gratitude. I've learned I don't have to practice being grateful for the situation I'm in to get the benefits, but just by being grateful in the situation.

Several years ago I was dating a man with children whose ex-wife was very much still in the picture. One day I found myself driving to the ex-wife's mother's home to meet with his ex-wife and her mother ... by myself. As I drove, I wondered how in the world I had gotten myself into this situation. I had no idea how this was going to go, but I definitely knew I was outnumbered and going into 'enemy' territory.

I remembered the concept of practicing gratitude. I started choosing to feel gratitude ... within myself, not for anything specific, just to feel gratitude as I was going through the experience. Somehow the visit went very well, and we all ended up leaving our time together feeling good. Who would have thought?! Afterward I could authentically practice gratitude for the situation as I drove home!!

If a healthy attitude helps our bodies become more healthy physically, then practicing gratitude seems a good choice!

For more information:

Relaxercise by David and Kaethe Zemach-Bersin, and Mark Reese
HarperCollins ISBN 0-06-250992-6

Vocal Power by Arthur Samuel Joseph
Vocal Awareness Institute   ISBN 978-1-588-72064-1

How to Use a Planner

I'm used to the Franklin-Covey planner, so I'll make suggestions that work with their system. If you use another system, just add sections to your planner to get the function. If you only use an electronic planner, find ways to incorporate these functions into your system, either electronically or on paper you carry with you.

When I'm spending most of my time in my home office, I can keep track of my appointments on my computer, and sync with my PDA to carry with me. When I go out, I add new appointments to my PDA and sync with my computer.

When I'm spending most of my time out of the office, meeting new people and attending meetings, I use my paper planner as well. It's just easier for me to take notes with pen and paper than to power up my PDA, find the right place and type one character at a time when I get a new phone number or information I want to remember. I keep this as auxiliary information, and when I get back to the office at the end of the day I review my notes and add them to my computer or PDA as appropriate, and then sync the PDA and computer.

Life used to be easier! If you don't need to keep track of certain details, don't worry about it. Organizational tools are there to make your life easier by helping you keep track of details that help you be more productive. If the planner is asking for something you don't need, just know it's there in case your circumstances change in the future. Use only the elements that help you now.

Elements (sections of your planner)

- **General**:
  - o Master task list (items with no specific time frame)
  - o Values & goals (see "Values-Based Time Management" 218)
  - o Focus (see "Focus Session" 198)
  - o Contacts
  - o Notes

- **Annual**:
  - o Calendar
    - this year
    - at least one year in the future
    - last year

- **Monthly**: (you may prefer weekly)
  - o Index
  - o Goals for this month

- **Daily**:
  - o Task list
  - o Appointment schedule
  - o Journal
  - o Expenses

Carry your planner with you everywhere. Develop a routine so you make sure you have it with you when you leave the house, your table at the restaurant, a meeting. It contains personal information like your wallet or purse, so keep track of it as you do your wallet or purse. As you go through the day, write down notes, phone numbers, and appointments all in one place ... your planner.

When I meet a new person and get their business card, I write their name, phone number, email and pertinent information in the contacts section. I keep the business card and file it at home in my "Contacts" file.

If I find out there is an upcoming meeting, or an agency or person to follow up with, I turn to the journal page for today, and write it there. I give it a title which I underline: Annual Meeting, and underneath I write the details. Then I go to the monthly index page, in the first column write today's date, and in the second column write "Annual Meeting". The index is wonderful! Three months from now I'll remember I wrote the annual meeting information somewhere, and I don't have to dig through my pile of papers, or go through each daily planner page. I can just look through a few monthly index pages until I find the listing, and then turn to the right daily page to find my notes.

If I'm at a meeting and I know I'll need several pages to take notes, I start a new page in the "Notes" section of my planner, and use as many pages as I like. I can move those pages to today's daily page, and make an entry in the monthly index so I can locate the notes later. Sometimes I type the notes into my computer later, and if so, I copy them into the "Notes" section of my PDA software so I have them electronically if I need them. But then I'm a techie. You may want to keep things more paper based.

It's important to prioritize your list of daily tasks, so you don't spend your valuable time getting pulled into a long-winded conversation about an item that is not your priority, or sometimes even your responsibility. Know where you're going today, and keep yourself on track. I prioritize using A, B, C and Z. I change priorities on my computer to Z when they are complete, because when I sort they go to the bottom of the list. Not all As are equal: use A1, A2, A3 etc. to further prioritize, so you know what to start with first.

Some of your priorities you can delegate to others. Keep them at the same priority level on your planner; just make a note of who you delegated to, and when they are supposed to do what.

If this gets very complicated, you might want to use project management software to keep track of specific projects with timelines and tasks that are dependent, meaning if someone is late getting back to you on their task, and other people are not able to start their part and the whole project becomes late, then you have a cascading effect on your plans for each task in the project. Let the project management software make the adjustments for you. See the "Project Management" section (213).

That's about it. The most important thing: Keep everything in one place, or at least somewhere you can find it again. When you reach for a piece of paper to write down some important bit of information, reach for your planner and write it there where you can find it easily.

Needs Literacy

Our human needs play an enormous role underlying every decision we make and everything we do. Sometimes it helps to get down to basics when we're trying to understand a situation, or to solve a problem.

Needs Hierarchy

Abraham Maslow organizes human needs into essential categories, one building upon the other:

• Physiological needs must first be met to sustain life: breathing, food, water, sex, sleep, homeostasis, excretion.

• Safety needs come next: security of body, employment resources, morality, the family, health, property.

• Love and belonging needs build upon the first two: friendship, family, sexual intimacy.

• Esteem is next: self-esteem, confidence, achievement, respect of others, respect by others.

• Self-actualization can be achieved after the preceding need categories are met: morality, creativity, spontaneity, problem solving, lack of prejudice, acceptance of facts.

Universal Human Needs

The Center for Nonviolent Communication uses needs as the basis for helping people in conflict understand each other. They list the following needs as being held by everyone. For complete list, see Needs Chart (page 233).

- Social connection
- Physical well-being
- Honesty
- Play
- Peace
- Meaning
- Autonomy

Needs-Based Communication Model

As taught by the Center for Nonviolent Communication:

1. **Observation**: Simply describe what a camera would see, without editorial filters of any kind.

2. **Feelings**: Guess what feelings the person may be experiencing (see the Feelings Charts 233) Note: If they correct you, that is a step forward in getting clarity. "I feel that ..." is not a feeling.

3. **Needs**: Guess what needs the person may be experiencing. Again, if they correct you, it's a positive step forward. "I need (person's name) to ..." doesn't count. What needs is the person speaking experiencing? (see the Needs Chart 238)

4. **Request**: Make a clear, present request, something doable in the moment. What exactly would that person want who to do now to get closer to what they want?

Conflict Resolution

Needs identification becomes very important in any negotiation. As you become more adept at identifying needs in yourself, you will become better at guessing what need the other person is trying to get met. In a conflict, you may discover you share the same need, or you each have needs that balance each other in some way. Bringing this awareness can make conversations and negotiations go much more smoothly.

Once each party can hear the authentic needs of the other party, strategies to get everyone's needs met often become obvious and easy. Often the conflicting parties are actually trying to get the same need met, and are simply approaching it with different strategies. When this becomes clear, we stop seeing the other party as an enemy, and our desire to reach out to another human being in pain motivates us to find solutions that work for everyone.

Needs Literacy Exercise:

To practice identifying needs in yourself and others, try making these lists when you have a quiet moment:

1. How you are most likely to speak to yourself when you are less than perfect? You probably speak to others this way, too.

2. What words or phrases come to mind when you're angry with others, or when you're judging them?

3. What stimulates defensive thoughts and hurt or angry feelings in you? Notice what the other person said, or what you thought they meant.

4. What are you most afraid that others might think of you?

As you look at your list, notice what feelings come up in you, and consider which of your needs might be met or unmet.

Whose Need?

During group conversations and meetings, it's helpful to keep track of whose need is on the table. Sometimes during a discussion a person's need gets met without having to achieve the strategy or end goal they originally brought into the conversation. Sometimes through thoughtful conversation at a need level, the entire paradigm of the conversation can shift as transparent sharing begins to illuminate an entirely new level of depth to the issue being discussed.

For more information:

www.cnvc.org

Open Space Technology

Harrison Owen created a largely leaderless and formless meeting methodology in 1985 which he calls Open Space Technology after discovering that attendees of his symposium reportedly enjoyed coffee breaks most. He decided to create his next symposium around coffee breaks.

He now spends about five minutes preparing for one to five day conferences which empower individuals to network and have significant conversations about topics of interest to the participants. This works for any size group. It is highly dynamic, very organic and has built-in flexibility in the moment.

Structure of the Event

The large group convenes. The facilitator briefly states the theme of the meeting, and invites participants to raise a related topic and announce it to the large group. These participants become the small group discussion leaders for the topic they have raised.

Someone writes each topic on an individual sheet of paper, which gets posted on a wall. The discussion leaders may agree to combine similar topics into a single small group.

When someone determines that posting on all issues is complete, times and places are set for the small group meetings of approximately one hour.

The discussion leader shows up to lead discussion. If no one else shows up, they consider the topic themselves. People may come and go during the course of the hour. There are four Principles and one Law of Open Space:

Four Principles

1. Whoever comes is the right people.
2. Whatever happens is the only thing that could have.
3. Whenever it starts is the right time.
4. When it's over, it's over.

The Law of Two Feet, or the Law of Mobility

"If at any time during our time together you find yourself in any situation where you are neither learning nor contributing, use your two feet. Go to some other place where you may learn and contribute."

For more information:

Open Space Technology: A User's Guide by Harrison Owen
Berrett-Koehler Publishers
ISBN: 978-1576750247

Project Management

The principles used by project managers can be useful when beginning any project. They involve strategies to organize and manage resources required to complete a project within defined scope, quality, time and cost constraints.

Project Steps

• First, define the project objective and the customer.

• Identify need, problem or opportunity and clearly define.

• Set goals, budget and expectations, including who supplies what, and approvals required by the customer. Payment terms, required schedule, evaluation criteria, availability of funds and resources throughout the life of the project. Consider competition, risk, mission, extension of capabilities, reputation, experience of key individuals, management capability, realism of schedule.

• Choose project(s) with the greatest benefit for the anticipated costs.

• Costs include labor, materials, subcontractors and consultants, equipment and facilities rental, travel, documentation, overhead, escalation, contingency or reserve, fee or profit.

• Select solution and define scope and deliverables, requirements, resources, type of contract. Get stakeholder and user involvement.

• Plan interdependent tasks, sub-tasks and sub-sub-tasks, resource needs and allocation, time requirements, track progress, review, make adjustments, report to stakeholders.

• Deliver solution, get customer approval, complete close-out activities, evaluate performance and invite customer feedback.

Tips

• Plan for the unexpected.

• User involvement is an important factor in project success.

• Become familiar with customers' business and needs.

• Manage the project team with respect and good communication.

Barriers to Effectiveness

Lack of clarity in terms of goals, roles definitions and responsibilities, project structure, commitment, communication, leadership, turnover, dysfunctional behaviors. Work scope, resource assignments, schedule, cost, priorities, organizational issues, personal differences.

Quality Cave Time

When life and work get busy and you feel pulled from all angles and don't know which way to turn ... take a moment to remember your favorite thing to do, and check your calendar to see how long it's been since you gave yourself any personal time.

Sometimes even five minutes can make a difference. If you can get by yourself where nothing is required of you for five minutes, it doesn't cost much time or any money to sit quietly with your eyes closed and imagine your dream vacation ... with you in the picture. Feel the sun on the beach, the cool mountain breeze, hear the wind in the sails, or the horse's gallop as you go riding. Just five minutes. We allow our bodies to experience plenty of stress as we imagine what might go wrong day to day; why not use this technique in reverse and imagine what we would like to go right!

How you get your quiet time is up to you. I just added this page to the book to remind you: You sometimes make better decisions when you're feeling fulfilled instead of depleted.

By the way, women need cave time, too!

Twelve Steps, Traditions, Concepts, Serenity Prayer

There is something valuable to be learned from a set of steps that has given hope and guidance to so many people in the midst of their very confusing and debilitating circumstances.

You can find myriad meetings almost everywhere of people who get together to focus on the principles behind the Twelve Steps to help them maintain sobriety, and mental and emotional balance. I'll highlight some of the principles that may translate into other ventures.

They are very clear on their purpose. They are only there to help each other recover from alcoholism. They are exclusive yet inclusive at the same time: The only requirement for membership is a desire to stop drinking. There are no experts; only fellow travelers improving their lives together. They are not allied with any sect or denomination, and they are only very loosely organized.

They study the Twelve Steps together to improve their individual lives. They admit they are not God, and affirm their willingness to learn and their interest in complete honesty, even when it means admitting something about themselves they may not like.

The Twelve Traditions guide their work as a group. Unity and their common welfare come first. The leaders are but trusted servants to speak for the membership, not to govern. They don't lend their name to any outside enterprise or cause, and they stay focused on their purpose of helping alcoholics get sober. They are self-supporting. As individuals they remain anonymous. They remind themselves to place principles above personalities.

The Twelve Concepts guide their organization as a whole. Each individual group is represented internationally. They avoid wealth and power, taking care not to place any member in a position of unqualified authority over others. They strive to remain democratic in thought and action. When a vote is taken, they take time to hear the minority opinion. When all voices are heard, the majority can then make better decisions to support the best interests of the overall organization.

The Serenity Prayer is quoted often:

"God grant me the serenity to accept the things I cannot change, courage to change the things I can, and wisdom to know the difference."

Values-Based Time Management

You've probably already slept through several time management courses. So have I. Here are some ideas to help time management work for you, and hopefully be more fun.

First, make life easier by keeping track of the paper and information that comes into your life. See "How to Use a Planner" (203) and "Finding Your Desk" (195). When you can see past your desktop and locate the time of today's meeting, you are out of survival mode and can begin thinking about self-actualization.

I keep a saying on my wall, "Nothing should be more highly prized than the value of each day" by Goethe. None of us knows how much time we have left, or under what condition tomorrow will find ourselves or our environment.

Going through life unconsciously may mean looking up one day and wondering where the last 20 years went. If I've gotten up each day for 20 years and decided not to plan and just let life happen, then okay. If I've let other people decide for me what is important in my life and how I should use my time and I wake up 20 years later, that is not so okay.

Consciously managing my time is a way of taking control of my own life. Starting from awareness of my values gives me power to control the direction of my life toward what matters to me, and what makes me happy.

Identifying Values

How do I know what my values are? I asked Nathaniel Branden that question, and he gave me some sentence completion exercises. You can find his entire program in the appendix of *The Art of Living Consciously*. I suggest you use the following questions to help you develop a list of values you would like to live by over the next year:

> One of the traits I look for in people is …
> One of the rules I try to live by is …
> I respect people most when they …
> I do not respect people when they …
> Sometimes I am drawn to people who …
> Right now it seems to me that …

> One of the principles that guides me is …
> One of the things I want out of life is …
> One of the things I want from people is …
> One of the things I want from work is …
> One of the things I expect of myself is …
> I am becoming aware …

> Life seems most fulfilling when …
> Life seems most painful when …
> I feel most alive when …
> I am beginning to suspect …

Nathaniel Branden
The Art of Living Consciously

What to Do Next

Ranking
Now that you have your list of values, rank them in order of importance to you.

Start with your most important value. Think about how the outcome of that value could manifest in your life by this time next year. Write a description of this, and include how you feel as you experience this positive outcome of what matters most to you. Make it about you and your experience, not about someone else's life.

• When you have the description, think about when, realistically, this might actually happen.

• Now make a list of the practical steps it would take to bring this about.

• Break them down into what has to happen monthly and weekly to make this happen.

Put Them Where You Can Find Them
Pull out your planner:

• Put these goals into your planner by month and week as appropriate.

• Now think about some task you can do every day to get closer to this goal.

• Put this task, or these tasks, on your daily pages, or a master task list that you look at every day.

• Put the description you wrote in Step 1 above in the "Focus" section of your planner so you can refer to it regularly.

Looking Deeper
Do this for each of your values, in order of priority.

Focus
Read "How to Use a Planner" to learn how to do a Focus Session
(198).

For more information:

The Art of Living Consciously by Nathaniel Branden
Simon & Schuster
ISBN: 978-0-684-81084-3

CHAPTER 15:
SECTION FIVE

Reference

Bibliography

Creativity

The Answer to How is Yes by Peter Block
Berrett-Koehler Publishers
ISBN 978-1-57675-271-5

Are You Ready to Succeed? by Srikumar S. Rao
Hyperion
ISBN 1-4013-0193-2

The Art of Possibility by Rosamund Stone and Benjamin Zander
Penguin
ISBN 0-14-200110-4

Cracking Creativity by Michael Michalko
Ten Speed Press
ISBN 978-1-58008-311-9

Creativity in Business by Michael Ray and Rochelle Myers
Doubleday
ISBN 0-385-25851-2

Flow: The Psychology of Optimal Experience by Mihaly
Csikszentmihalyi
HarperPerennial
ISBN 0-06-092043-2

The Personal Mastery Program by Srikumar S. Rao
Discovering Passion and Purpose in Your Life and Work
Sounds True Audio Learning Course

224

Education

The Compassionate Classroom by Sura Hart, Victoria Kindle Hodson
Puddledancer Press
ISBN 978-1892005069

The No-Fault Classroom: Tools to Resolve Conflict & Foster Relationships Intelligence by Sura Hart and Victoria Kindle Hodson
Puddledancer Press
ISBN 978-1892005182

Leadership

Beyond Counterfeit Leadership by Ken Shelton
Executive Excellence Publishing
ISBN 1-89009-20-2

Blueprint to a Billion by David G. Thomson
Wiley
ISBN 978-0471747475

Built to Last: Successful Habits of Visionary Companies by Jim Collins and George I. Porras
Collins Business
ISBN 978-0060566104

The Five Most Important Questions You Will Ever Ask About Your Organization by Peter F. Drucker with Jim Collins, Philip Kotler, James Kouzes, Judith Rodin, V. Kasturi Rangan, Frances Hesselbein
Leader to Leader Institute
ISBN 978-0470227565

Good to Great by Jim Collins
HarperCollins
ISBN 0-06-662099-6

Good to Great and the Social Sectors by Jim Collins
Collins Business
ISBN 978-0-9773264-0-2

Hesselbein on Leadership by Frances Hesselbein
Jossey-Bass
ISBN 978-0787963927

In Search of Leadership: How Great Leaders Answer the Question 'Why Lead?' by Phil Harkins and Phil Swift
McGraw-Hill
ISBN 978-0071602952

In Search of Quality edited by Ken Shelton
Executive Excellence Publishing
ISBN 0-9634-9174-1

Integrity at Work edited by Ken Shelton
Executive Excellence Publishing
ISBN 1-890009-32-6

The Leader of the Future 2 edited by Frances Hesselbein, Marshall Goldsmith
Leader to Leader Institute
ISBN 978-0-7879-8667-4

Leadership: A Behavioral Science Approach by Dr. Paul Hersey and Ron Campbell
Center for Leadership Studies, Inc.
ISBN 0-931619-09-2

The Leadership Challenge by James M. Kouzes and Barry Z. Posner
Jossey-Bass
ISBN 978-0787984922

Management of Organization Behavior by Paul H. Hersey, Kenneth H. Blanchard, and Dewey E. Johnson
Prentice Hall
ISBN: 978-0131441392

A New Paradigm of Leadership edited by Ken Shelton
Executive Excellence Publishing
ISBN 1-890009-18-0

On Leadership by John W. Gardner
Free Press
ISBN 978-0029113127

The Organization of the Future 2: Visions, Strategies, and Insights on Managing in a New Era by Frances Hesselbein, Marshall Goldsmith
Jossey-Bass
ISBN 978-0470185452

Political Dilemmas at Work by Dr. Gary Ranker, Colin Gautrey, Mike Phipps
John Wiley & Sons
ISBN 978-0-470-27040-0

Riding into the Sunrise by Al Quie
Pogo Press
ISBN 978-1880654453
Succession: Are You Ready? by Marshall Goldsmith
Harvard Business School Press
ISBN 978-1422118238

What Got You Here Won't Get You There by Marshall Goldsmith
with Mark Reiter
Hyperion
ISBN 978-1-4013-0130-9

The Wisdom of Teams by Jon R. Katzenbach and Douglas K. Smith
HarperBusiness
ISBN 0-06-0522000-3

Management

The 7 Habits of Highly Effective People by Stephen R. Covey with
Ken Shelton
Simon & Schuster
ISBN 978-0-7432-6951-3

Differences Do Make a Difference by R. Roosevelt Thomas Jr, Tracy
Irving Gray Jr, Marjorie Woodruff
American Institute for Managing Diversity
ISBN 978-0963234209

Getting Things Done by David Allen
Penguin
ISBN 0-14-200028-0

Health Promotion in the Workplace by Michael P. O'Donnell
Delmar Thomson Learning
ISBN 0-7668-2866-2

Love 'Em or Lose 'Em by Beverly Kaye and Sharon Jordan-Evans
Berrett-Koehler Publishers, Inc
ISBN 978-1-57675-327-9

What Happy Companies Know by Dan Baker, Cathy Greenberg,
Collins Hemingway
Prentice Hall
ISBN 0-13-185857-2

Personal Development

The Art of Living Consciously by Nathaniel Branden
Simon & Schuster
ISBN: 978-0-684-81084-3

Change Your Brain, Change Your Life by Daniel G. Amen, M.D.
Random House
ISBN 0-8129-2998-5

Empowerment Takes More Than a Minute by K. Blanchard,
Carlos & Randolph
Berrett-Koehler Publishers
ISBN 1-881052-83-4

The Magic of Thinking Big by David J. Schwartz
Simon & Schuster
ISBN 0-671-64678-8

Mojo: How to Get It, How to Keep It, and How to Get it Back
When You Need It! by Marshall Goldsmith
Hyperion
ISBN 978-1401323271

The One Minute Entrepreneur by Ken Blanchard, Don Hutson
Executive Books
ISBN 978-1-933715-30-8

Outliers by Malcolm Gladwell
Little, Brown
ISBN 978-0-316-01792-3

Relaxercise by David Zemach-Bersin, Kaethe Zemach-Bersin and
Mark Reese
HarperCollins
ISBN 0-06-250992-6

Self-Esteem at Work by Nathaniel Branden
Jossey-Bass Publishers
ISBN 0-7879-4001-1

The Six Pillars of Self-Esteem by Nathaniel Branden
Bantam
ISBN 0-533-37439-7
Taking Responsibility by Nathaniel Branden
Simon & Schuster
ISBN 0-684-83248-8

Talent is Overrated by Geoff Colvin
Penguin Porfolio
ISBN 978-1-59184-224-8

Vocal Power by Arthur Samuel Joseph
Vocal Awareness Institute
ISBN 978-1-588-72064-1

Voice of a Leader CD set by Arthur Samuel Joseph
Sounds True
ISBN: 978-1591795636

Your Money or Your Life: Transforming Your Relationship with *Money* ... by Vicki Robin, Joe Dominguez, and Monique Tilford
Penguin
ISBN 978-0143115762

Sales

Get Clients Now! by C. J. Hayden
Amacom
ISBN 0-8144-7992-8

Selling the Invisible by Harry Beckwith
Warner Books
ISBN 0-446-52094-2

Stand Out! Branding Strategies for Business Professionals by Simon Vetter
July Publishing
ISBN 978-0970430373

You, Inc.: The Art of Selling Yourself by Harry Beckwith and Christine Clifford Beckwith
Business Plus
ISBN 978-0446578219

Feelings Chart

Feelings when your needs <u>are</u> satisfied:

AFFECTIONATE
compassionate
friendly
loving
open hearted
sympathetic
tender
warm

CONFIDENT
empowered
open
proud
safe
secure

ENGAGED
absorbed
alert
curious
engrossed
enchanted
entranced
fascinated
interested
intrigued
involved
spellbound
stimulated

INSPIRED
amazed
awed
wonder

EXCITED
amazed
animated
ardent
aroused
astonished
dazzled
eager
energetic
enthusiastic
giddy
invigorated
lively
passionate
surprised
vibrant

EXHILARATED
blissful
ecstatic
elated
enthralled
exuberant
radiant
rapturous
thrilled

GRATEFUL
appreciative
moved
thankful
touched

HOPEFUL
expectant
encouraged
optimistic

JOYFUL
amused
delighted
glad
happy
jubilant
pleased
tickled

PEACEFUL
calm
clear headed
comfortable
centered
content
equanimous
fulfilled
mellow
quiet
relaxed
relieved
satisfied
serene
still
tranquil
trusting

REFRESHED
enlivened
rejuvenated
renewed
rested
restored
revived

Feelings when your needs are not satisfied:

AFRAID
apprehensive
dread
foreboding
frightened
mistrustful
panicked
petrified
scared
suspicious
terrified
wary
worried

ANNOYED
aggravated
dismayed
disgruntled
displeased
exasperated
frustrated
impatient
irritated
irked

ANGRY

enraged
furious
incensed
indignant
irate
livid
outraged
resentful

AVERSION

animosity
appalled
contempt
disgusted
dislike
hate
horrified
hostile
repulsed

CONFUSED

ambivalent
baffled
bewildered
dazed
hesitant
lost
mystified
perplexed
puzzled
torn

DISCONNECTED

alienated
aloof
apathetic
bored
cold
detached
distant
distracted
indifferent
numb
removed
uninterested
withdrawn

DISQUIET

agitated
alarmed
discombobulated
disconcerted
disturbed
perturbed
rattled
restless
shocked
startled
surprised
troubled
turbulent
turmoil
uncomfortable
uneasy
unnerved
unsettled
upset

EMBARRASSED

ashamed
chagrined
flustered
guilty
mortified
self-conscious

FATIGUE

beat
burnt out
depleted
exhausted
lethargic
listless
sleepy
tired
weary
worn out

PAIN

agony
anguished
bereaved
devastated
grief
heartbroken
hurt
lonely
miserable
regretful
remorseful

SAD

depressed
dejected
despair
despondent
disappointed
discouraged
disheartened
forlorn
gloomy
heavy hearted
hopeless
melancholy
unhappy
wretched

TENSE

anxious
cranky
distressed
distraught
edgy
fidgety
frazzled
irritable
jittery
nervous
overwhelmed
restless
stressed out

VULNERABLE
fragile
guarded
helpless
insecure
leery
reserved
sensitive
shaky

YEARNING
envious
jealous
longing
nostalgic
pining
wistful

Needs Chart

The following list of needs is neither exhaustive nor definitive. It is meant as a starting place to support a process of deepening self-discovery and to facilitate greater understanding and connection between people.

CONNECTION

acceptance
affection
appreciation
belonging
cooperation
communication
closeness
community
companionship
compassion
consideration
consistency
empathy
inclusion
intimacy
love
mutuality
nurturing
respect/self-respect
safety
security
stability
support
to know and be known
to see and be seen
to understand and be understood
trust
warmth

PHYSICAL WELL-BEING

air
food
movement/exercise
rest/sleep
sexual expression
safety
shelter
touch
water

HONESTY

authenticity
integrity
presence

PLAY

joy
humor

PEACE
beauty
communion
ease
equality
harmony
inspiration
order

AUTONOMY
choice
freedom
independence
space
spontaneity

MEANING
awareness
celebration of life
challenge
clarity
competence
consciousness
contribution
creativity
discovery
efficacy
effectiveness
growth
hope
learning
mourning
participation
purpose
self-expression
stimulation
to matter
understanding

Follow-up

I'd love to read your comments and experiences with the concepts presented in the book. Send me an email at Marilyn@CoachMarilyn.com or find me at www.twitter.com/marilynmcleod.

You'll also find the complete bibliography in this book online. I'll continue adding new books and resources as I find them.

If you've appreciated the book and would like to leave a review on your favorite online retailer, I would be grateful!

If you'd like to find a support community around the concepts of this book, please visit my website: http://www.CoachMarilyn.com. I value your contributions to the conversation about success in business and in life!

Your fellow traveler,

Marilyn McLeod
Marilyn@CoachMarilyn.com

Exercise Worksheets

I don't know about you, but I like efficiency, so I thought I'd make it easier for you and give you some pages to write on in this book.

Getting Started
How to Use This Book

1)   Decide how you are going to use this book:

  • Reference book when you need new ideas
  • Study guide by yourself or with your coach
  • Improvement guide for your team, family, support group

2)   Create time in your schedule to follow through with your intention above

3)   Is there anything in the way of you following through? If so, address this as best you can to support the improvement you want.

4)   Send me an email occasionally to let me know how it's working for you! You will find the book website at http://www.CoachMarilyn.com.

CHAPTER 1:

Recession or Plenty

1) Make a list of your current reality: One list of what you like about your life and business now, and the other list of what you don't like.

2) Look honestly at both lists, and begin to create a vision of what you truly want that resonates deeply with the truth of who you are.

3)   Step out of any mental constructs such as anger,
      judgment, criticism, diagnosis, blame and resentment.
      From that point of clarity, look at your 'don't like' list
      again. Are there people and resources on that list who
      could help you if you approached them in a positive,
      supportive way?

4)   Write down any new perspective you now have about
      your own definition of recession and plenty.

CHAPTER 2:

Success

1)   Write down your own definition of success. Now think of someone who loves you unconditionally, without regard to your material or social success. From their perspective, read the definition you have just written down. Does it ring true as your own?

2)   Do an experiment to find out more about yourself.
      Think about something you have strong feelings about,
      and then ask some people for their ideas about this
      topic. Watch how you respond. Do you notice yourself
      reaching for a pen to write down the new ideas you are
      learning, or do you hear yourself defending your deeply
      held convictions?

3)   If you heard yourself talking defensively, stop and notice
      what you are saying to yourself right now. Are you
      berating yourself for doing something wrong, or are
      you giggling in loving amusement because you caught
      yourself doing something silly again?

CHAPTER 3:

Ownership

1) Think about yourself and your reasons for wanting to be in business. Write down your thoughts.

2) Think about who you want to share ownership with, and why. Write down what you expect each owner to contribute, and what you think the business owes them. Beyond the money, are there intangibles involved?

3) Think about the functions you expect your enterprise will require to run. Which functions are supplied by an owner, and which will you hire out? Try to clarify everything.

4) Look at the list of people you plan to involve in your enterprise. How much do you really trust them? Have they demonstrated integrity and dependability in the past? In what ways can you not count on them?

5) Now look at yourself and apply the same standards to yourself. Can you really count on yourself to carry out your part of this business? Make a list of improvements you would like to see in yourself and everyone else involved before you move forward.

CHAPTER 4:

Image

1) Can you convey your message effectively without PowerPoint?

2) The next time you are in front of a prospective customer or stakeholder, notice how you are coming across:
   a. Do you push your 30 second commercial at them whether they want it or not? When you do this, how often does this lead to a new customer?
   b. Do you listen first to understand who you are talking to and what they need? When you do this, how often does this lead to a follow up conversation?

3) Ask people around you (who will tell you the truth) how often you let them win, and whether they consider you a good listener.

4) Think about your presentation from your ideal customer's point of view. What about image would turn them on, and what would turn them off?

CHAPTER 5:
Legacy

1)   Try Marshall Goldsmith's exercise: 95 year old man or woman (see page 110)

2)   Think about what matters to you and your customers and stakeholders. Is there a contribution you can make to your local community to address a need in this area?

3)   Think about where you came from, and how people still in that situation may be struggling. Is there something you can do to make life easier for them, or to help them succeed?

4)   Think about what you have learned during your life and career. Is there something you can package and turn into a gift or product that could help others?

CHAPTER 6:
You

1) Think about you and what really makes you happy. Write down specifics that come to mind.

2) Think about times you feel stifled, discouraged, uncomfortable. Write down the situations that stimulate this feeling, and what specifically you don't like about it.

3)   Think about yourself and all that you are. What aspects
      of yourself that make you happy remain untapped?

4)   If you could have an ideal day, an ideal job, an ideal
      customer, an ideal life, what would it be like? Dream,
      and take notes!!!

CHAPTER 7:
Customers

1) Think about who you enjoy spending time with. Write down any specifics that come to mind.

2)   Are there particular activities you enjoy doing with these people, and others that you don't like doing with them? Think about this and take notes.

3)   What kind of people do you naturally attract? Are they people you enjoy being with? If yes, what do you like about them? If no, what don't you like about the interaction? Can you think of a way to make this win-win? Take notes.

CHAPTER 8:
Business

1) Spend time with people you enjoy, doing activities you enjoy. While you are doing this, listen for clues about services or products they value and don't have, or needs that are not being fulfilled. Take notes.

2) Look at your list and take some time to consider what your favorite people need and want that you could provide.

3)   Put together some ideas and talk with some of your prospects about them. Get their involvement and buy-in. If they think it's a bad idea, ask other people. If they think it's a great idea, ask if they know anyone else who might be interested.

4)   Test by having an entry-level offering to sell that does not cost you very much to provide, and gives your customer an experience of your product or service. Then you can see how committed they are to actually buying the solution they said was so valuable to them.

CHAPTER 9:

Focus

1)   Make a list of everything you need to keep track of in a spreadsheet program.

2)   Add a column to the left, and label it "category". Add a category to each line item.

3)   Add a new column to the left, and label it "activity". For each item, type 'email', 'phone', 'visit', 'research', etc.

4)   Add another column immediately to the left of the large item description column. Label this one 'priority', and assign a priority to each line item. You can use A, B, C, and A1, B3, even Z for those you decide don't need to be on the list right now, or if they are already completed.

5)   You can now sort this list by priority, activity, and category. Add other columns as needed.

6)   Make a backup copy of this, and use it as a working document, making changes as you think of new items, as priorities change, and as you check things off the list.

CHAPTER 10:
Sales

1)   Look at your promotional materials and messages in
        various mediums.

        Are they consistent?

        Are the claims accurate?

        Are you using benefit statements?

        Do they address the needs of your target audience?

        Do they look and sound attractive and compelling to
        your target audience?

2)   Really listen to your customers. Find out how they heard about you. Do more of that.

3)   Ask your happy customers for referrals.

CHAPTER 11:
Follow-up & Delivery

1) Ask your customers about their experience with you. Tell them you would like to improve, and ask if they have any suggestions.

2) Remember to just listen without any judgment or hurt feelings. Keep in mind, you are sincerely interested, and the only way to find out is to ask. Take notes.

3) Thank them for their candor and willingness to share.

CHAPTER 12:
Review & Celebrate

1) Stay on top of market changes in your industry.

2) Constantly ask yourself if this affects your business, or if it could in the future.

3) Make notes about possible strategies that you can refer to as needed in the future.

4)   Make changes if needed.

5)   Make sure you have at least some fun every day, so you stay lighthearted and inspired.

6)   Think about your customers and do something to add fun, pleasure or appreciation to their day.

Index

How do you use an index? It's intended to be an easy way to find references to a particular word within the text of the book. Another use I recommend you try is to use it as an idea-generator as you're thinking through an issue. Just let your mind wander as you browse through these words, and see if any associations give you new ideas to help your project or process along.

Symbols

A

D

dance 122, 124-7, 141
dangerous 146
day off 91
death 38, 97
December 24, 67-8
decision 52, 76, 86, 114, 155-6, 158, 207
defensive 57, 209
define 5, 14, 99, 213
definitions 13, 214
delegate 67, 205
deliverables 213
delivery 15, 84, 115
de Mille, Rosalind xi, 124, 127-8
democracy 41
denial 97
dependability 20, 24
depleted 215
desk 35, 61-2, 99-100
despair 35, 97, 126
destiny 22
details 65, 67, 69, 73, 76, 93, 203, 205
developing leaders 164
Devi, Indra 126
de Vos, Rich xvi
Diaghilev, Sergei 125-6
diagnosis 2
dialog 34
disappointment 97, 126
discouraged 15, 47
disdain 29
distance 85, 200

documentation 213

dogs 99

domestic chores 101

dream 1, 170, 187, 215

Drucker, Peter F. xiii, 41, 43, 144, 150-1, 163-4, 149

drugs 67

dysfunctional behaviors 214

E

easy xxi, xxii, 14, 32, 67, 78, 99, 121, 209

economic collapse 23

economy 3, 160, 185

education 40-1, 97, 159, 173

email xxiv, 65, 76, 78, 180, 204

Emerson, Ralph Waldo 189

empty 104-5

endurance 200

enemy 10, 202, 209

energy 16, 57, 69-70, 74, 97, 112, 114, 155

engine 41, 47

enjoy xxi, 15, 17, 45, 48, 50-1, 55, 56, 59, 61, 91, 93, 99, 108, 117, 120, 180, 195

entrepreneur 15

environment xviii, xxvii, 3, 7, 22, 31, 52, 89, 94-7, 100, 103, 110, 146, 195, 218

equipment 6, 99, 213

escalation 213

evaluate 214

excitement 57, 104

excuses 19, 154

exercise 21, 33, 35, 50, 70, 104, 152, 180, 190, 200

expenses 101, 119

expensive 19, 134, 171

experience xi-xxiv, 10, 20, 22, 28, 48, 55, 60-2, 83-4, 93, 95, 99,
    118-119, 121, 138, 141, 170-1, 186, 159, 198, 202, 213,
    215, 220
expert 53, 63, 144, 177
expertise 21, 24, 63, 75, 159
extra 9, 88, 95, 98, 100, 106, 120, 131-2, 138-9, 201

F

facilities 138, 213
fact 88, 140, 185
fail 24, 90, 123, 141
family xxiii, 5, 10, 16, 21, 24, 49, 56, 94, 97, 101, 103, 105-6,
    113-115, 118, 126, 129, 132, 134, 136, 138, 189, 192, 207
family business 21, 24
fans 48
fee 213
feedback 60, 83, 84, 103, 214
Feed*Forward* xiv, 85, 152-3, 180-2
feeling xxiii, 3, 5-6, 10, 47, 52, 57, 96, 101, 105, 118, 160, 171,
    176, 189, 190, 202, 208, 215
Feldenkrais 201
file 60, 69, 195-6, 205
financial 112, 114, 126, 171, 193
flexibility 61, 200, 211
flier 74-5
floss 199
focus xxvi, 2, 40, 49, 66, 73, 97, 98, 103, 106, 113-114, 123,
    131, 139, 153, 193, 201, 216
follower readiness 158
follow up 28, 78, 180, 205
fool 16
football 109-110, 177
force 38

G

I

J

K

L

M

N

nature 50, 143, 192

neatness xxi, 28

need ii, xviii-xxvi, 9, 17, 24, 28, 33-5, 42, 52, 56, 57, 59-60, 63, 66, 78, 84-6, 88-9, 95-100, 103, 109, 118, 131, 140-1, 150, 152, 154, 159-161, 177, 184-5, 195, 203, 205, 207-210, 213, 215

negative xxvii, 16, 84, 97-8

neglect 22, 69, 129

negotiation 209

network 24, 62, 75, 192, 211

new business 15, 23, 45, 74, 81, 88, 104, 185

New York City 41

next step 7, 75, 79, 86, 103, 119

NFL 109

Nijinski 125, 126

nutrition 200

O

objective 19, 213

obligations 189

office hours 61

Office of Economic Opportunity 39

sonline xxvi, 62, 77-8, 155, 180

online marketing 77

open heart 10, 85

Open Space Technology 211-212

opinion 84

opportunities xvii, 4, 42, 49, 88, 95, 98, 113, 120-1, 126-7, 159, 171, 188

Oprah xvi, 86

options xvi, xxiv, xxvi, 4, 51, 69, 109, 114, 120, 134

optometrist 109

organize 69, 113, 150, 195, 213

other woman 10

outcome 15, 188, 219

overhead 113, 193, 213

Owen, Harrison 211, 212

ownership 19, 24, 150

P

pain 67, 75-6, 99, 209

painting 99, 124

Panzram, Ms. Violet 35-6

paradigm 210

parent 20, 136

partnership 19, 24

part time 104

patterns 120, 168

Pavlova, Anna xvi, 124

payoff 168

PDA 203, 205

peer 180-1

peer coach xxvii, 180-3

perception 84, 95

perfect xiv, xv, 62, 91, 105, 110, 209

performance 34, 52, 63, 110, 126, 158, 160-1, 177, 214

Phipps, Mike 169, 227

physical 124, 139, 199

pioneer 20, 126, 132-3

plan xxvi-xxvii, 20, 24, 38-9, 88, 91, 101-3, 108, 130, 150, 168-9, 192, 200, 218

planner 198, 203-6, 220

pleasure xiv, 87, 92, 199

plenty 3, 11, 23, 50, 93, 129, 132, 137, 144, 200-1, 215

polite 78

politics 8

Q

Quaker 36
Quie, Al xvi, 227
quiet xxi, 35, 66, 97-100, 184, 198, 201, 209, 215

R

rain 3, 4
Randolph, Alan 229
Rangan, V. Kasturi 43, 151, 225
rank 219
Ranker, Gary xiv, 7, 9, 31, 168-9, 227
Rao, Srikumar S. xiv, 170-2, 185-7, 224, 187
rapport 63, 76, 85
Ray, Michael 224
readiness 150, 161
realistic 60, 136, 155, 160
reality 2, 15, 34, 90, 106, 146, 160-1
recession 3, 11, 93
recovery xxi, 96-7, 99
Reese, Mark 202, 230
reference xxv, 3-4, 15, 49, 178
Reiter, Mark 154, 157, 228
relationship 24, 84-6, 120, 158, 182-3
relevance 76
remember xxvi, 4-7, 15-16, 29, 37-8, 60, 68, 84, 86, 95, 100, 106, 129, 131, 136, 182, 189-190, 201, 203, 205, 215
Remisoff, Nicolas 126
rental 213
report 102, 106, 198, 213
reputation 79, 110, 125, 213
requirements 213
research 65, 89, 102-4, 106-7
resentment 2, 96

S